THE ADVENTURES OF AKBAR

FLORA ANNIE STEEL

1st WORLD
LIBRARY
Literary Society

The Adventures of Akbar

Flora Annie Steel

© 1st World Library, 2009
PO Box 2211
Fairfield, IA 52556
www.1stworldlibrary.com
First Edition

LCCN: 2009923408

Softcover ISBN: 978-1-4218-8832-3
Hardcover ISBN: 978-1-4218-8931-3
eBook ISBN: 978-1-4218-8733-3

Purchase *"The Adventures of Akbar"*
as a traditional bound book at:
www.1stWorldLibrary.com/purchase.asp?ISBN=978-1-4218-8832-3

1st World Library is a literary, educational organization
dedicated to:

- Creating a free internet library of downloadable ebooks

- Hosting writing competitions and offering book publishing
scholarships.

Interested in more 1st World Library books? contact:
literacy@1stworldlibrary.com
Check us out at: www.1stworldlibrary.com

1ˢᵗ World Library Literary Society

Giving Back to the World

"If you want to work on the core problem, it's early school literacy."

> **- James Barksdale, former CEO of Netscape**

"No skill is more crucial to the future of a child, or to a democratic and prosperous society, than literacy."

> **- Los Angeles Times**

"Literacy... means far more than learning how to read and write... The aim is to transmit... knowledge and promote social participation."

> **- UNESCO**

"Literacy is not a luxury, it is a right and a responsibility. If our world is to meet the challenges of the twenty-first century we must harness the energy and creativity of all our citizens."

> **- President Bill Clinton**

"Parents should be encouraged to read to their children, and teachers should be equipped with all available techniques for teaching literacy, so the varying needs and capacities of individual kids can be taken into account."

> **- Hugh Mackay**

A DEDICATION

Oft when the house lay silent in the heat
My thoughts would be so full of you, my sweet,
That dreaming half—I seemed to hear once more
Your little fingers fluttering at the door,
The pitter patter of your childish feet
In joyous rhythm cross the echoing floor.

Then small, soft hands would nestle into mine,
And warm soft arms around my neck would twine,
As soft and warm the dream child on my knees,
Cuddling so close in clear young voice would tease
And tease and tease in mimicked glad young whine
For "Just one little story if you please."

So half in jest and half in earnest, too,
Mostly I think to dream my dreaming true,
I'd conjure up long tales of lands afar
And days gone by that yet remembered are;
Shaping my stories with this end in view
To gain the verdict "Tell some more, Mamma."

For I was happy when I had beguiled
Into my life the spirit of a child.
Thus one by one the weary hours flew
And page by page a little volume grew,
So—that my dreams with truth be reconciled,
Take it, my darling, it was writ for you.

April, 1875

Long years have sped since that poor book was penned.
None read the pages. Therefore at the end
Of this world's life I dedicate to two
Small boys—her sons—whose question'ng eyes of blue
Tell me that dreams of childhood never end
This book. So take it boys—'twas writ for you.

1911

CONTENTS

PREFACE

This book is written for all little lads and lasses, but especially for the former, since it is the true—*quite* true—story of a little lad who lived to be, perhaps, the greatest king this world has ever seen.

It is a strange, wild tale this of the adventures of Prince Akbar among the snowy mountains between Kandahar and Kabul, and though the names may be a bit of a puzzle at first, as they will have to be learned by and bye in geography and history lessons, it might be as well to get familiar with them in a story-book; though, indeed, as everybody in it except Roy the Rajput, Meroo the cook boy; Tumbu, the dog; and Down, the cat (and these four *may* have been true, you know, though they have not been remembered) really lived, I don't know whether this book oughtn't to be considered real history, and therefore

A LESSON BOOK

Anyhow, I hope you won't find it dull.

CHAPTER I

FAREWELL

Bismillah Al-la-hu Akbar!

These queer-looking, queer-sounding words, which in Arabic mean "thanks be to God," were shrilled out at the very top of Head-nurse's voice. Had she been in a room they would have filled it and echoed back from the walls; for she was a big, deep-chested woman. But she was only in a tent; a small tent, which had been pitched in a hurry in an out-of-the-way valley among the low hills that lead from the wide plains of India to Afghanistan. For Head-nurse's master and mistress, King Humayon and Queen Humeeda, with their thirteen months' old little son, Prince Akbar, were flying for their lives before their enemies. And these enemies were led by Humayon's own brothers, Prince Kumran, Askurry and Hindal. It is a long story, and a sad story, too, how Humayon, so brave, so clever, so courteous, fell into misfortune by his own fault, and had to fly from his beautiful palaces at Delhi and wander for years, pursued like a hare, amid the sandy deserts and pathless plains of Western India. And now, as a last resource, his followers dwindled to a mere handful, he was making a desperate effort to escape over the Persian border and claim protection at the hands of Persia's King.

So the poor tent was ragged and out at elbows, for all that it was made of costly Kashmir shawls, and that its poles were silver-gilt.

But Head-nurse's "Thanks be to God!" came from a full heart.

"What is it? What *is* it?" called an anxious voice from behind the curtain which divided the tent in two.

"What?" echoed Head-nurse in high glee. "Only this: His Imperial Highness, Prince Akbar, the Admired-of-the-World, the Source-of-Dignity, the Most-Magnificent-Person-of-the-Period—" She went on, after her wont, rolling out all the titles that belonged of right to the little Prince, until the soft, anxious voice lost patience and called again, "Have done— have done; what is it? Heaven save he hath not been in danger."

Head-nurse, stopped in her flow of fine words, sniffed contemptuously. "Danger! with me to guard him? No! 'Tis that the High-in-Pomp hath cut his first real back tooth! He can eat meat! He has come to man's estate! He is no longer dependent upon milk diet." Here she gave a withering glance at the gentle looking woman who was Baby Akbar's wet-nurse, who, truth to tell, was looking just a little sad at the thought that her nursling would soon leave her consoling arms.

"Heavens!" exclaimed the voice from within, "say you so?" And the next instant the curtain parted, and there was Queen Humeeda, Baby Akbar's mother, all smiling and eager.

Now, if you want to know what she was like, you must just think of your own dearest dear mummie. At least that was what she seemed to little Prince Akbar, who, at the sight of her, held out his little fat arms and crowed, "Amma! Amma!" Now, this, you will observe, is only English "Ma-Ma" arranged differently; from which you may guess that English and Indian children are really very much alike.

And Queen Humeeda took the child and kissed him and hugged him just as any English mother would have done. Head-nurse, however, was not a bit satisfied with this display of affection. That would have been the portion of any ordinary child, and Baby Akbar was more than that: he was the heir apparent to the throne of India! If he had only been in the palaces that belonged to him, instead of in a miserable tent, there would have been ceremonials and festivities and fireworks over this cutting of a tooth! Aye! *Certainly* fireworks. But how could one keep up court etiquette when royalty was flying for its life? Impossible! Why, even her determination that, come what might, a royal umbrella must be held over the blessed infant during their perilous journeys had very nearly led to his being captured!

Despite this recollection, as she listened impatiently to the cooings and gurglings, she turned over in her mind what she could do to commemorate the occasion. And when pretty Queen Humeeda (thinking of her husband, the king, who, with his few followers, had ridden off to see if a neighboring chief would help them) said, "This will be joyful news wherewith to cheer my lord on his return," Head-nurse's irritation found voice.

"That is all very well," she cried. "So it would be to any common father of any common child, Your Royal Highness! This one is the Admired-of-the-Whole-World, the Source-of-Dignity, the Most-Magnificent-Person-of-the-Period—"

And she went on rolling out queer guttural Arabic titles till Foster-mother implored her to be silent or she would frighten the child. Could she not see the look on the darling's face?

For Baby Akbar was indeed listening to something with his little finger up to command attention. But it was not to Head-nurse's thunderings, but to the first long, low growl of a coming storm that outside the miserable tent was turning the distant hills to purple and darkening the fast-fading daylight.

"Frighten?" echoed Head-nurse in derision. "The son of Humayon the heroic, the grandson of Baber the brave could never be frightened at anything!"

And in truth the little lad was not a bit afraid, even when a distant flash of lightning glimmered through the dusk.

"Heavens!" cried gentle Queen Humeeda, "his Majesty will be drenched to the skin ere he returns." She was a brave woman, but the long, long strain of daily, hourly danger was beginning to tell on her health, and the knowledge that even this coming storm was against them brought the tears to her eyes.

"Nay! Nay! my royal mistress," fussed Head-nurse, who, in spite of her love of pomp, was a kind-hearted, good woman, "this must not be on such an auspicious day. It must be celebrated otherwise, and for all we are so poor, we can yet have ceremonial. When the child was born were we not in direst danger? Such danger that all his royal father could do in honor of the glad event was to break a musk-bag before his faithful followers as sign that the birth of an heir to empire would diffuse itself like perfume through the whole world? Even so now, and if I cannot devise some ceremony, then am I no Head-nurse!"

So saying she began to bustle around, and ere long even poor, unhappy Queen Humeeda began to take an interest in

Flora Annie Steel

the proceedings.

A mule trunk, after being ransacked for useful odds and ends, was put in a corner and covered with a worn satin quilt. This must do for a throne. And a strip of red muslin wound about the little gold-embroidered skull cap Baby Akbar wore must, with the heron's plume from his father's state turban, make a monarch of the child.

In truth he looked very dignified indeed, standing on the mule trunk, his little legs very wide apart, his little crimson silk trousers very baggy, his little green brocade waistcoat buttoned tight over his little fat body, and, trailing from his shoulders in great stiff folds, his father's state cloth-of-gold coatee embroidered with seed pearls.

So, as he always wore great gold bracelets on his little fat arms, and great gold jingling anklets fringing his little fat feet, he looked very royal indeed. Very royal and large and calm, for he was a grave baby with big, dark, piercing eyes and a decided chin.

"He is as like his grandfather as two splits of a pea!" cried Head-nurse in rapture, and then she went to the tent door and shrilled out:

"Slaves! Quick! Come and perform your lowly salute on the occasion of the cutting of a back tooth belonging to the Heir-to-Empire, the Most—"

She cut short her string of titles, for a crash of thunder overhead warned her she had best be speedy before the rain soaked through the worn tent.

"Quick, slaves!" she added; "keep us not waiting all day. Enter and prostrate yourselves on the ground with due reverence! Quick! Quick!"

She need not have been in such a hurry, for it did not take long for the "slaves," as she called them, to perform their lowly salaam by touching the very ground with their foreheads. There were but three of them—Old Faithful, the trooper; Roy, the Rajput boy; and Meroo, the scullion; the rest were away with their master, King Humayon.

Old Faithful, however, tall, lank, grey-bearded, brought enough devotion for half a dozen followers. He had served with little Akbar's grandfather, Babar the brave, and when he saw the child standing so fair and square, he gave almost a sharp cry of remembrance and delight. And when he stood up after his prostration, in soldier fashion he held out the hilt of his old sword for the baby to touch in token that its service was accepted. Queen Humeeda, who stood beside her little son, guided his fat fingers to the sword; but at the very moment a vivid flash of lightning made her give a shriek and cover her face with her hands. But little Prince Akbar having got a hold of the hilt, would not let go. And to Old Faithful's huge delight he pulled and pulled till the sword came out of the scabbard.

"An omen! An omen!" cried the old man. "Like his grandfather, he will fight battles ere he be twelve!"

Then there was Roy, the Rajput lad, whom the royal fugitives had found half dead from sunstroke in the wide, sandy Rajputana deserts, and whom, with their customary kindness, they had succoured and befriended, putting him on as a sort of page boy to the little Heir-to-Empire. He was a tall, slim lad for his twelve years, was Roy, with a small, well-set head and a keen, well-cut face. And his eyes! They were like a deer's—large, brown, soft, but with a flash in them at times.

Flora Annie Steel

For the sunstroke which had so nearly killed the lad had left his mind a little confused. As yet he could remember nothing of what had happened to him before it, and could not even recollect who he was, or anything save that his name was Roy. But every now and again he would say something or do something which would make those around him look surprised, and wonder who he could have been to know such things and have such manners.

After him came Meroo, the misshapen cook-boy. He was an odd fellow, all long limbs and broad smiles, who, when his time arrived, shambled forward, cast himself in lowliest reverence full length on the ground and blubbered out his delight—now that the princely baby could really eat—at being able to supply all sorts of toothsome stews full of onions and green ginger, to say nothing of watermelons and sugar cane. These things, strange to say, being to little Indian children very much what chocolate creams and toffee are to English ones.

So far all had gone well, and now there only remained one more salute to be made. But little Adam, who was Head-nurse's own son, and who had hitherto been Baby Akbar's playmate, refused absolutely to do as he was bid. He was a short, sturdy boy of five, and nothing would induce him to go down on his knees and touch the ground with his fore-head. In vain Meroo, the cook-boy, promised him sweets if he would only obey orders; in vain Old Faithful spoke of a ride on his old war-horse, and Roy, who was a most wonderful story-teller, promised him the best of all, Bopuluchi. In vain his mother, losing patience at such a terrible piece of indecorum, rushed at him and cuffed him soundly. He only howled and kicked.

And then suddenly Baby Akbar, who had been listening with a solemn face, brought his little bare foot down on the mule trunk with such a stamp that the golden anklets jingled and jangled, and his little forefinger went up over his head in the real Eastern attitude of royal command.

"Salute, slave, salute," he said with a tremendous dignity. And there was something so comical about the little mite of a child, something so masterful in the tiny figure, something so commanding in the loud, deep-toned baby voice, that every one laughed, and somehow or other Adam forgot his obstinacy and made his obeisance like a good boy.

And then once more pretty Queen Humeeda hugged and kissed her little son, and all the rest applauded him, and made so much of him that he began to think he had done something very fine indeed, and crowed and clapped his hands in delight.

But the merriment did not last long, for there was a clatter of horses and swords outside the tent.

"My husband!" cried Queen Humeeda in a flutter. "What news does my lord bring?"

CHAPTER II

THE FIRST VICTORY

The next moment a tall, handsome man entered the tent; but one look at his pale, anxious face was enough to tell those inside that the news was bad. So for an instant there was silence; and in the silence, with a deafening roar and a blinding blaze of blue light, came a terrific crash of thunder followed by a sudden fierce pelt of hail upon the taut tent roof.

It sent a shiver through the listeners. They felt that the storm had broken indeed upon their heads, that danger was close beside them.

Then the King stepped to his wife's side and took her hand, and as he spoke there was a sob in his breath as of an animal who after a long chase finds himself at last driven to bay.

"Come!" he said briefly, "there may yet be a chance for us. My horse, weary though it be, will suffice for thy light weight. In the mountains lies possible safety. Come! There is not a moment to lose."

"But—but the child—" faltered the Queen.

King Humayon's voice failed him. He could not speak for a

moment; but he shook his head.

"I will not leave the child—" began the wretched mother. "My lord! thou canst not have the heart—"

"It is his only chance—" interrupted the poor King, his face full of grief and anger, of bitter, bitter regret—"His only chance of life! In the mountains yonder, with winter snow upon us, lies certain death for one so young. Were we to stay with him here, he would find death with us—for my brother Askurry is close behind us. But if we are gone, God knows, but he might spare the child. Askurry is not all unkind, and the little lad favors my father so much that his blessed memory may be safeguard. God send it so. It is his best chance, his only chance. So come—"

"I cannot! I cannot!" moaned the poor mother distractedly.

"There is no other way, sweetheart!" said the King, "so be brave, little mother, and come for thy son's sake. He will be safer here than with thee. Come! trusting in God's mercy for the child. And come quickly while the darkness of the storm shrouds our going."

Then he looked round on those others—Head-nurse, Wet-nurse, Old Faithful, Roy the Rajput, and Meroo the cook-boy—not much of a bodyguard for the young prince, and yet, since force would be useless, perhaps as good as any other, if they had a head between them. But the nurses were women, Faithful nothing but an old soldier, and the two others were mere boys. Some one else must be left. Who? Then he remembered Foster-father, Foster-mother's husband. He was the man. Solid, sober, clear-headed. So, as Queen Humeeda was being hurriedly wrapped in a shawl by the two weeping nurses, he gave them a few directions. They were to stay where they were, no matter what happened, until Foster-father returned from showing the fugitives a path he knew to the mountains, and then—

King Humayon could say no more. Only as, after a hurried, tearless, hopeless farewell to his little son, he paused at the tent door to take a last look, his half-fainting wife in his arms, he said suddenly in a sharp, loud voice:

"Remember! In your charge lies the safety of the Heir-to-Empire."

The words sank into the very hearts of those who stood watching the group of hurrying figures making its way rapidly toward the hills.

"Pray Heaven," muttered Old Faithful anxiously, "that they be over the rise before those who follow see them."

So they stood fearfully watching, watching. And Heaven was kind, for though one great blue blaze of lightning showed the fugitives clear against the sky line, when the next came there was nothing but the rugged rocks.

Then for the first time Baby Akbar, who had been silent in his nurses' arms, watching with the rest, lifted up his deep-toned baby voice:

"Daddy, Amma," he said contentedly, "gone up in a 'ky."

Whereupon Foster-mother wept loudly and prayed that good angels might protect her darling.

But Head-nurse was more practical, and set about considering how best that safety might be secured. Who was there who could help? No one of much use, truly, though every one was brimful of devotion and ready to give his or her life for the Heir-to-Empire.

"I will kill the first man who dares—" began Old Faithful.

"Aye! The first! But how about the last, old man?" interrupted Head-nurse. "Force will be of no avail. Askurry hath half an army with him."

"Harm shall only come to the child through my body," wept Foster-mother, whereat Head-nurse laughed scornfully.

"Woman's flesh is a poor shield, fool! God send we find better protection than thy carcass."

"Boo! hoo!" blubbered Meroo the cook-boy. "Lo! Head-nurse! I could kill a whole army by poisoning their suppers."

Head-nurse nodded faint approval. "Now, there is some sense in that, scullion, but what about that they may do supperless? If they should dare—"

"They will not dare," said a clear, sharp voice, and Roy the Rajput lad stepped forward, a light in his great eyes. "My mother used to say, 'Fear not! A king's son is a king's son always, so be that he forgets not kingship.'"

Head-nurse stood puzzled for a second, then she caught the meaning of the lad's words, for she was a clever, capable woman, and had all a woman's quickness.

"Thou art right, my lad," she said slowly, looking curiously at Roy, from whose face the flash of memory seemed to have passed. "Thou art right. In royalty lies safety. The Heir-to-Empire must receive his enemies as a King! Quick! slaves! Close the tent door and let us bring forth all we have, and make all things as regal as we can. There is no time to lose."

And they did not lose any. The result being that when, quarter of an hour afterward, Prince Askurry, bitterly disappointed at finding that his real quarry, the King and Queen, had escaped, strode with some of his followers into the tent where he was told Baby Akbar was to be found, he paused at the door, first in astonishment and then in amusement.

It was really rather a pretty picture which he saw. To begin with the tent had been lit up with the little rushlight lamps they call in India *chiraghs*—tiny saucers which can be made of mud in which a cotton wick floats in a few drops of oil— and a row of these outlined the mule trunk throne. Then Meroo's misshapen limbs had been hidden under a chain corselet and helmet, so he made quite a respectable fellow to Old Faithful, as the two supporters stood bolt upright with drawn swords one on either side, while beneath them, on the ragged old Persian carpet which had been spread to hide the dirty tent drugget, crouched Head-nurse and Foster-mother, their faces veiled with their best gold embroidered veils.

A great pile of cushions had been placed on the muletrunk, and in the centre of these sat Baby Akbar, the Royal heron's plume of his turban waving gently in the breeze caused by the slow dignified sweep of the Royal fan which Roy, who stood behind his young master, was swinging backwards and forwards.

But it was not the prettiness of the picture which made Prince Askurry pause. It was the child's open fearless face which reminded him at once—as King Humayon had hoped it might—of that dear, beloved father whose memory, even in their worst wickednesses, was ever a good influence in the lives of his sons. Babar the Brave! Babar of the Generous Heart! the Kindly Smile! Who could forget him?

But behind Prince Askurry were others who did not

remember; who were eager to kill and have done with Humayon and his son for ever.

And when they saw Prince Askurry pause, they were quick with advice.

"It is unwise to spare snakes' spawn," said one.

"The boy is father to the man," said another. "He who is wise kills young rats as well as old ones."

And still Prince Askurry paused while poor Head-nurse and Wet-nurse went sick with fear under their veils at what might be going to happen, and Old Faithful's hand clasped the hilt of his sword tighter, since come what may he meant to strike one blow for his young master. But Roy's keen eyes showed —as the peacock's feather fan swept past them backwards and forwards—like a hawk's as it hovers above a partridge. There was in them a defiance, a certainty that victory must come.

Suddenly a wicked laugh filled the tent. "Peace! brothers," said a sneering voice, "Prince Askurry prefers to leave the snake to fight with his own son in the future."

The taunt told. It was true! Better to scotch the snake now, than to leave it to be dangerous by and by; dangerous perhaps to his own little son who was but a few years older than Baby Akbar.

Prince Askurry strode forward drawn sword in hand; but whether he really meant to use it or not cannot be told, for a very strange thing happened. Baby Akbar had been listening to the fierce voices just as he had listened to the angry voices when Adam had refused to salute. And now he saw some one before him who appeared to have no intention—as

Flora Annie Steel

Adam had no intention—of making his reverence; so, remembering the fine thing he had done when the latter had been naughty, up went the little hand again, and once more the loud, deep, baby voice said imperiously:

"Salute! Slave! salute!"

The words were barely uttered when by pure chance Prince Askurry's foot caught in the ragged carpet, and—?

And down he came flat as a pancake on the floor in the very lowliest salute that ever was made!

The next moment, however, he sat up, half-stunned, and looked wrathfully at his little nephew.

But Baby Akbar's honest open face was full of grieved sympathy.

"Poor, poor!" he said, shaking his quaintly crowned head, "tumbu down. Nanna kiss it, make it well."

Prince Askurry sat stupidly staring for a moment or two. Then the memory of many a childish hurt cured by like gracious offer from his father came back to him, making his heart soft. He sprang to his feet and waved by his councillors to cruelty.

"Go, my lords!" he cried fiercely. "Go seek the King who is no true King if ye will, and kill him. But this boy goes with me to Kandahar; the stuff of which he is made counts for life, not for death."

Then with a sudden generous impulse, for he was at heart his father's son, he held the hilt of his drawn sword in token of vassalage for Baby Akbar to touch.

And the child, clever, observant beyond his years, remembering how his mother had guided his fingers to Old Faithful's weapon, put out his little hand solemnly and touched it.

Behind their close-folded veils Head-nurse and Wet-nurse wept for joy. And the old trooper's grip relaxed and the hard relentless look faded from Roy's face.

For here was safety, for a while at any rate, for the Heir-to-Empire.

He, and Fate between them, had won his first victory. No! his second, since the first had been the conquering of Adam's obstinacy.

But for that Baby Akbar might not have behaved with such dignity.

CHAPTER III

THE ROYAL UMBRELLA

That night even Roy the Rajput, who as a rule woke every hour to see to his little master's safety, slept sound. And so did the others, though they sat up till Foster-father crept in to the tent about midnight, after having seen the Royal Fugitives safely over the Persian border. Of course, there was nothing but miles on miles of snowy mountains before them, nothing but long struggle and privation to be hoped for; still they were out of India, out of an enemy's country. For which Heaven be thanked!

So they wrapped themselves in their quilts and lay down to rest with hearts eased for the time of immediate anxiety.

Head-nurse, however, began at once, after her wont, to make plans for resuming some of the courtly ways which hurry had made impossible. The gold embroidered royal red umbrella was one thing she was determined to have.

But who was to hold it over the Royal Infant? Roy would get tired of it during a long march. He was but a boy; and after all there should be a Deputy, Assistant, Second, Umbrella Bearer to Majesty.

Could Meroo, properly dressed, of course, be promoted to the position?

She actually woke Foster-father from his well-earned first sleep to propound this knotty question.

"Good woman," he murmured patiently, "make what court appointments ye will. Create the scullion Prime Minister, so I have my sleep."

And he was snoring almost before the words were out of his mouth.

So next morning Head-nurse, refusing the baggage camel with panniers which Prince Askurry sent for the use of the little Heir-to-Empire, organised a procession of her own.

First of all came Foster-father, stout and solid, on his skew-bald hill pony which was called Horse-chestnut because it was patched all over, like an unripe chestnut, with yellow, brown and white.

It had a lovely tail that touched the ground, and a coat that was long and wavy like an Irish setter's. A wise, sober pony was Horse-chestnut; he never attempted to climb up anything he thought too difficult, but just gave a look at it to make sure and then put down his head calmly, and began to graze until his rider found an easier path.

Next came Trooper Faithful on his old white charger Lightning. Once upon a time it had been like its name, swift exceedingly, but now, like its master, it was slow and stiff.

Then followed Head-nurse, astride, in Indian fashion, the bay Belooch mare which had been Queen Humeeda's favourite mount until it had had to be left behind in one of the hasty

Flora Annie Steel

moves which had of late been so common in the hunted life of the Royal Fugitives. The mare, of course, had been taken by the pursuers, and brought along with them; and the groom in charge of it had come grinning with delight to Foster-father when he found himself in the same camp again. Foster-father was for riding the bay mare himself and giving sober Horse-chestnut to the Heir-to-Empire, but Head-nurse would not hear of this. The bay mare was, she said, altogether more royal. So there she was, with Baby Akbar astride a cushion in front, perched on the skittish creature, feeling at heart very nervous, for she was but a poor rider. However, she held on very tight with one hand, held Baby Akbar still tighter with the other, and trusted to Providence, while Roy and Meroo ran beside her on either side, alternately holding up the Royal Umbrella as best they could.

Foster-mother on a mule, with little Adam perched in front of her brought up the rear of the procession. It was a poor one for progress even along the levels, because of the bay mare's fidgeting and caperings, but when the steep hill sides were reached it became impossible to keep up with the rest of the equipage. So Prince Askurry and his men pushed on ahead leaving the little party alone, since escape was impossible on that wild mountain road, especially with the rear guard of the camp coming a few miles behind them. And, indeed, if such an idea had entered the heads of any of the party it must soon have fled before the difficulty of getting along at all. It was a steep zig-zag path, and looking upwards you could see it zigging and zagging right away to the sky line. Poor Foster-mother, who came last, could not take her eyes off it, for the bends immediately above her were filled with the most terrifying sights. First her stout husband, who seemed to be in the act of slipping over Horse-chestnut's tail. On the next Old Faithful, driven to dismounting and laboriously lugging Lightning up by the bridle. But the last zig-zag in front of her called forth piercing shrieks. For the bay mare, not having been ridden for some time, was full of beans. Baby Akbar insisted on holding the reins, and Meroo, whose turn it was to hold the umbrella, *would* slip and slither among the stones, thereby bringing its fringe right on the bay mare's nose.

"Oh! Head-nurse, have a care! The blessed child!" shrieked poor Foster-mother as a more than usually bad stumble sent the umbrella on to the mare's tail.

This was too much for it. Frightened out of its senses, it gave a frenzied bound forwards, then rearing straight up, hung over the edge of the path, as if it meant to take a downward plunge.

All seemed lost! Foster-father and Faithful stood petrified with despair. Meroo would have dashed forward to catch at the rein but Roy, knowing with that curious instinct of his, that that would only make matters worse, as it would still further frighten the mare, held him back by main force. The only person who was not spellbound with fear was Baby Akbar. He thought it a fine joke that his mount should stand up on its hind legs and paw the air. So he shrieked with delight, and dropped the reins to clap his hands, as he always did when he was pleased. Now this was the very best thing he, or anybody else, could have done. The mare, feeling herself free, thought better of it, and wheeling round dropped her fore feet on the path once more.

Foster-father's loud Arabic thanksgiving ended in an equally loud order. "Get off the mare, woman. Horse-chestnut is the only mount thou art fit for. Roy! carry that foolish umbrella behind."

"In front—the emblems are ever carried in front," protested Head-nurse feebly.

"I said behind," was all the answer she got, and behind it went while they toiled up and up.

After a while the road became surprisingly bad; nothing in fact but a watercourse, and Foster-father began to doubt if they could be on the right way. Possibly, when they were all excited over the mare's bad behaviour, they had taken a wrong turning. But as the path led ever upwards, he judged it better to go on, though it was terribly hard work. Every moment the road became worse and worse until it ceased to be more than a mere ladder of rocks which puzzled even Horse-chestnut. More than once he stopped dead and would no doubt have refused any further attempt to climb had there been anything at which to graze. But there was nothing; nothing but rocks. So, after a pause he made the best of a bad bargain, raised himself on his hind legs, sought a foothold for his fore feet in some crevice, and then scrambled up. Only the two children enjoyed themselves, Baby Akbar laughing with delight and clapping his hands over all the slips and slitherings which even nimble Horse-chestnut made, and which reduced Head-nurse and Wet-nurse to piteous wails to Roy not for Heaven's sake to let go of the Heir-to-Empire's baggy trousers. And Adam enjoyed himself, also, running on in front and making snowballs in the drifts which, ere long, were to be seen sheltering from the sun in the clefts of the rocks.

The sight of them made Foster-father frown. "We go too high," he said. "Heaven send we have not to climb to a higher pass."

His remark made Head-nurse give way altogether. She wept loudly, saying in that case she had better stay and die where she was, thus saving them the trouble of carrying her down the hill.

At that very moment, however, Adam who had run far ahead began waving his arms and shouting:

"He says 'The top! the top!'" cried Roy, who was keen in hearing as in everything else. "Courage, mother! our troubles are over!"

They had not *quite* ended, but in a few minutes more they had reached the beginning of the pass proper. Before them lay a grassy boggy slope curling gently upwards between higher rockier slopes. A little stream plashed softly adown it, through a perfect wilderness of flowers, and without one word the tired travellers threw themselves beside it for rest and refreshment.

But Baby Akbar looked a little troubled.

"Amma, Dadda 'way 'way in a 'ky," he said solemnly, and essayed to crawl on over the grass. For he could not walk yet, though he spoke so well. They say he began to talk when he was nine months old.

Flora Annie Steel

CHAPTER IV

TUMBU-DOWN

After a while the party started on their way once more feeling greatly brisked up. But the heat of the day was now upon them, and though the snow lay close beside the path, the fierce sun melting it made the vapour rise and turned the narrow valley into a regular steam bath.

The perspiration ran down the travellers' faces and especially down poor Head-nurse's; for she had insisted on taking off her veil to twist it turbanwise round Baby Akbar's head since the Royal Umbrella was forbidden. Foster-mother had tried to take off hers also, but Head-nurse had angrily forbidden her to do any such thing. If she, Head-nurse, died of sunstroke what matter, but if Foster-mother failed, what—even though one back tooth had been gloriously cut—would become of the Heir-to-Empire, the Admired-of-the-World, the Great-in-Pomp, etc.?

So, to comfort herself she went on mumbling titles as she struggled along, the sun beating fiercely on her bare head. Such a quaint head, with sleek black hair parted and plaited and hung with jewels, even down the long pigtail of brown wool that was added on to the back to make the hair look more plentiful.

It was a piteous sight and Foster-mother was so conscious of the devotion it meant that she said "Lo! Head-nurse, thou art a good, good soul though a hard one to me; but I will never, never, never, forget this day."

"Nor I," groaned Head-nurse, "but 'tis for the Heir-to-Empire."

It was a full hour before the slope ended in a level bog, on the other side of which began a visible descent. Then in the angled hills a blue shadow began to rise, telling of a valley below them.

"Bismillah!" (Thanks be to God) cried Foster-father piously. And every one echoed the remark except Baby Akbar. He turned round and looked back at the snowy peaks which were beginning to show behind them.

"Amma, Dadda 'way 'way mountains," he said regretfully and his little mouth went down as for a cry, when every-body's attention was distracted by the sudden appearance of a huge furry black dog which came bounding down the hill side, its big white teeth gleaming as it uttered shrill, sharp, growling barks.

Head-nurse and Foster-mother shrieked with fright, little Adam ran like a hare for the shelter of his mother's petti-coats, and Meroo the cook-boy, remembering his bare legs—for like all Indian scullions he wore short cotton drawers—squatted down where he was standing, in order to protect them. Even Roy, brave boy that he was, looked uncom-fortable, and both Foster-father and Old Faithful whipped out their swords.

These were not needed, however, for the next instant a wild-looking figure clad in a brown blanket started up from behind a rock and shouted to the dog. It stopped instantly, but stood still—snarling, though obedient.

It was the funniest looking dog you can imagine. Bigger than a big collie, it was furry all over even to its tail. And it was black as ink. In fact with its tiny prick ears and small sharp pointed muzzle all lost in a huge soft black ruff and nothing to be seen but red tongue, white teeth and beady black eyes, it was a regular golliwog of a dog.

When Foster-father saw the man in the brown blanket, who from his crook was evidently a shepherd, he heaved a sigh of relief. "Now," he said, "we shall be able to find out our way."

But he was mistaken. The man did not understand a word they said, neither could they understand a word he said.

Head-nurse was in despair. "He speaks like a ghost of the desert," she wept. "We shall all die of starvation before he understands."

"Die?" echoed Foster-father stoutly. "Not so, woman! There is one language all understand."

Whereupon he placed himself right in front of the shepherd, opened his mouth wide and then shook his head. Next he pointed to his stomach and shook his head again. Finally he began to chew violently, rubbed his stomach and grinned.

The shepherd grinned too and rubbed *his* stomach, where-upon Foster-father turned triumphantly to Head-nurse.

"Said I not sooth, woman," he asked. "Hunger hath a tongue of its own, and all men know it."

Once begun, signs soon brought so much understanding,

that, whistling to his dog, the shepherd started down the hill at a great pace, beckoning them to follow.

"Not so fast, friend, not so fast!" panted Foster-father, "we be not all born on a mountain as thou art. And there are women and children, too." He pointed to poor Head-nurse and Foster-mother, who were indeed dropping with fatigue, and the man seemed to understand, for he pulled up. But he had to keep some way off because his dog, who kept close as a shadow to his master's heels, never ceased growling. So they tramped on wearily until just below them they saw a *marg* or mountain upland, where some goats were grazing. One part of this dipped down into a little valley, and there, in the shelter of some huge rocks, they saw two or three small brown blanket tents, such as shepherds use on the Beluchistan hills. They were just like waggon tilts only not so large.

Here, at any rate, was prospect of food and rest, and the poor travellers brisked up again. But alas! between them and the tents lay a formidable obstacle. Nothing less than a birch-twig bridge over a rushing stream which filled up the bottom of a wide rift or chasm in the upland. This chasm stretched right across the upland from a steep rock which blocked up the head of the little valley, and out of which the stream gushed, and there was no way of crossing it, so the shepherd explained by signs, except the birch-twig bridge. Now a birch-twig bridge is a very terrifying thing to anybody who is not accustomed to them. It is simply a strong flat plait of birch twigs about nine inches wide which is flung from one side to the other, and which, of course, droops and sags like a rope in the middle. Into this plait are stuck every few feet or so cross sticks, and to these sticks a rope is fastened as a sort of hand rail. Across such a bridge as this the hill children walk as easily as an English child does over a great brick span; but Head-nurse resolutely refused to set foot over it herself, much less to allow the Heir-to-Empire to risk his neck on such an appallingly dangerous structure. In vain Foster-father, in order to set a good example, allowed himself to be led over by the shepherd with his eyes carefully bandaged lest he should get giddy in the middle by looking down. As a matter of fact, this only made Head-nurse more frightened, for, of course, the bridge swung and swayed with the weight of the men on it. She would sooner, she declared, try to climb Heaven on a rainbow! That was at least steady. Roy tried to hearten her up by walking over himself with open eyes, though he felt frightfully dizzy and had to fling himself flat on the grass to recover when he did get over. Then Meroo, blubbering loudly that he was going to his death for his young master, climbed up on the shepherd's back and allowed himself to be carried over just to show how easy it was.

It was all in vain! Head-nurse was firm. They must bring the tents to the Heir-to-Empire; the Heir-to-Empire should not go across a tight rope to the tents. And there she would have remained had not a great, tall burly woman with a fat baby on her hip come out of one of the tents, and grasping the position, stalked over the bridge without even touching the hand rail, caught Baby Akbar from Foster-mother, who was too taken aback to resist, set him on her other hip and calmly stalked back again, leaving the two women too surprised and horrified even to scream.

But when they saw the Heir-to-Empire safe on the other side, they consented to be carried across pick-a-back.

So there they were before long eating goats' milk cheese fried like a beefsteak and drinking long draughts of a sort of sour milk.

One of the shepherds could speak a little Persian, and from

him Foster-father, to his great relief, learned that Prince Askurry's camp was only a mile or two down the valley, so, feeling certain of being able to reach it before sundown, he called a halt, and they all lay down to rest in one of the tents, Baby Akbar between his two nurses for safety sake. For one could never tell, Head-nurse remarked, what might happen amongst people who spoke the language of ghosts in the desert, and kept such strange animals. A great golliwog of a black dog who sat on one side of the tent like an image, watching them as if he meant to eat them, and a great fluff of a white cat sitting on the other with her eyes shut as if she did not want to watch them.

No! Indeed it was impossible to tell what might not happen!

And that is exactly how it turned out. What *really* did happen no one knew. It was Foster-mother who, waking first, let loose a shriek while still half awake. This roused Head-nurse, who let loose another. For Baby Akbar was no longer between them. The Heir-to-Empire had gone—had disappeared—was not to be found!

Roy was out of the tent in a second, treading in his haste on Meroo, who was sleeping outside, and who began to howl confusedly. Old Faithful fumbled for his sword, Foster-father rubbed his eyes as if *they* must be at fault.

But there was no Baby! And what is more, both the black dog and the white cat had disappeared also; at least they were no longer on the watch.

Never was there such a commotion. The rocks resounded with cries and every one searched everywhere; even in the great tall basket panniers in which hill shepherds carry their goods and chattels.

Flora Annie Steel

But not one sign of the little fellow was to be found, until—horribly, dreadfully, near to that awful birch-twig bridge—Foster-mother seized on a tiny gold-embroidered skull cap that was lying on the grass.

"It is his!" she sobbed, "it is my darling's! He hath tried to get to the mountains to his Amma, and he hath fallen from that accursed cats' cradle. He is dead! He is killed!"

Every face, except the shepherds', who did not, of course, understand what was said, turned pale. It was indeed possible, perhaps probable, that the faithful little soul, who remembered when others forgot, had tried—

It was a terrible thought. But the shepherds, seeing the cap, at once whistled to their dog, and the one who spoke Persian explained that if it were shown the cap it would take up the track of the child at once.

But though they whistled and whistled no dog came.

Then the shepherds began to look grave and mutter among themselves.

"What are they saying? What gibberish are they talking?" shrilled poor Head-nurse, trying to keep hope alive by being angry. The man who spoke Persian looked at her cheerfully.

"Only that perhaps the dog has eaten the child. We keep it hungry that it may chase the wild animals."

This was too much for the womankind. They simply rent the air with heartbroken sobs.

But Foster-father, grave and silent, would not give up hope. Every foot of the ravine must be searched, first downwards, as, had the child really fallen into the stream it must have been carried with it. Then as a last forlorn hope upwards. So, peering down carefully from either side, they traced the ravine till, gradually becoming shallower, less steep, it merged into the grassy valley. But there was no sign. Then sadly they commenced their upward search, until they were close to the high cliff whence the stream gushed out. Here they found that the ravine was wider, and at the bottom of it a patch of sand and boulders showed that there was foothold beside the roaring torrent.

"I will climb down and see if there is aught," said Roy; "it is easier here—if he had fallen here, he might—" the tears in his voice prevented more, as he tucked up his garments preparatory to the difficult descent.

But the shepherds raised an urgent outcry. There was a demon in the cavern, they said, whence the water came. There was no use angering it, no use in losing another life.

Roy struggled madly in their detaining hands, but Old Faithful and Foster-father looked at each other. Whether there was a demon or not it was a risk to another life and that should not be a young one.

"No, boy!" said the old warrior stoutly. "This is my task, not thine. I am good swordsman to begin with, and demons—if there be any—like not a clean sword thrust. Also I have been pilgrim to Holy Mecca and demons—if there be any—like not pilgrims' flesh."

So, muttering prayers and holding his drawn sword in his teeth, since both hands were needed for the parlous descent, he commenced his task while the others watched him eagerly.

　　　　　　Flora Annie Steel

About half way down he paused, looked up and called back; but they could not hear what he said.

"Take thy sword out of thy mouth, man," shrieked Head-nurse almost beside herself with grief and rage; "it isn't manners to speak with the mouth full."

True enough, but Old Faithful had some difficulty in obeying orders. However, he managed to steady himself for a moment on his two feet; so sword in hand he bawled back.

"'Tis true! There *is* a demon. It growls. I hear it plainly. Farewell! I go on, secure in my sword and Holy—"

Here a foot slipped and he went sliding, slithering, slipping down to the bottom where, happily only bruised, he sat half-stunned staring in front of him.

And then there echoed up to the listeners the most terrible barking, and yelping, and growling, and spitting, that ever was heard!

"The demon! The demon!" yelled the shepherds in terror, and ran for their lives.

But Roy, ear over the cliff, listened for a second, and the next had followed Old Faithful. Foster-father was not long behind him, and Meroo was close on his heels. Foster-mother and Head-nurse were not to be left out, and somehow they all managed to get down in safety.

And then they all stood and sat silent and agape with surprise and delight.

For what they saw was this. A low cavern in the rock, and on a shelving bank of dry sand Baby Akbar sitting up and rubbing his eyes, while on one side of him was the golliwog of a black dog, his fur all bristling, his white teeth gleaming as he filled the air with furious barks; while on the other was the white fluff of a cat, her back arched, her tail the size of two, spitting and growling fiercely.

How had he got there? Foster-father looked at Foster-mother, Head-nurse looked at Old Faithful, and Roy looked at Meroo, and they all looked at each other.

But Baby Akbar only put out one fat hand towards the black dog and said "Tumbu," and the other fat hand towards the cat and said "Down," and that was all he would say.

He had tumbled down; but how, when, and where, and how the dog and the cat came to be with him no one ever knew from that day to this.

Flora Annie Steel

CHAPTER V

ON THE ROAD

Naturally when, after an uneventful journey with the shepherd as guide, they reached Prince Askurry's camp that evening, they came to talk over the incident. Foster-father was not sparing of Head-nurse. The whole tissue of misfortunes, which had ended in Baby Akbar so nearly losing his life—and that he had been spared was simply a miracle—arose from her insisting on a Royal Procession. But for that, both she and the child would have gone comfortably on a camel. They would have kept up with the other baggage animals and none of the distressful events would have happened. It should not, however, happen again. Of course, Head-nurse tried to brazen it out and assert that the Heir-to-Empire could always count on a miracle in his favour; but in her heart-of-hearts she knew that Foster-father was right.

So next morning she said nothing when she saw a camel with two panniers kneeling in front of the tent, ready for its load. *That* had to be endured, but she revenged herself by objecting to the black dog and the white cat, who sat expectantly one on either side, evidently prepared for a start.

"Whose are those uncouth beasts?" she asked of Roy angrily. "Did I not tell those ghosts of the desert who call themselves shepherds to remove them last night? Why have they come back? Take them away! Catch them! Tie them up! Such mean born animals have no right to attend the Mighty-in-Pomp, the Lord-of-Light," etc., etc.

She rolled out the titles sonorously, determined that if she was docked of dignity in one way she would have it in another.

Now it was not very hard to catch the big black golliwog of a dog, even though he did snarl and snap and try to bite. There were a lot of camp followers who were only too glad to have the amusement of capturing him, so, after a very short space poor "Tumbu," for Baby Akbar insisted on calling him so, was being dragged off at the end of a long rope to his masters the shepherds, looking very sad, with his tail between his legs.

But it was quite different with "Down," the cat. She had made up her mind to stay where she was, and it is very hard, indeed, to make a cat change its mind when it is once made up.

So she moved about gently, from one place to the other, purring softly and looking as mild as milk, her blue eye—for real Persian cats often have their eyes of different colours and one of them is always blue—ever so friendly, as if she were just longing to be picked up. Only the very tip of her bushy tail swayed a little, and that is a sure sign that a cat is contrary. And contrary Down was. The very instant any one tried to pick her up—why! she was somewhere else!

Head-nurse ere long joined in the chase, saying all the rest didn't understand cats. But she soon lost patience and declaring that she had never been done by a dumb animal yet, started capture by force. A circle was formed round the point where Down sat blinking in the sunlight, and shawls and veils were held up to make it complete. Then step by step they advanced towards the cat, who, in truth, viewed the enclosing wall with polite indifference. It was really rather a funny sight to see stout Head-nurse without her veil tip-toeing in line towards pussy and shrilling out her orders to the others to close in and be sure to leave no loopholes. Step by step her voice became more and more triumphant, and it really seemed as if the cat *must* be caught this time, for Down sat sweetly purring until she was actually hidden from sight behind the high-held screening cloths.

"Now then! quick!" shrilled Head-nurse. "Close in—close—"

But her order ended in a scream of fright, for there was pussy in one flying leap on her bare head, scrabbling up her scanty hair, and with another away up the hillside leaving nothing but claw-marks behind her!

Head-nurse wept with angry tears; but Foster-father, always sensible, said "Enough! cry on the camel if you will, but now is the time to slip away before the obstinate animal can return."

There was wisdom in this; therefore Head-nurse composed herself comfortably in one pannier while Foster-mother, who was lighter, settled into the other with Baby Akbar. So off they set at the dignified lollop which camels affect, and Head-nurse began to congratulate herself on having success-fully evaded the "uncouth beasts."

But there is no counting on cats. If they are here one moment and gone the next, they are also gone one moment and here the next. So, as the camel was passing under a thorn tree about half a mile out from camp, a great fluff of white hair sprang from the branches and landed right in Head-nurse's broad lap. And there was Mistress Down looking as if butter wouldn't melt in her mouth, and purring away like a kettle on the boil.

Head-nurse gave in *altogether* then. "When a cat really makes up its mind," she said with forced wisdom, "it is little use any one else making up theirs!"

So pussy sat in her lap, and after a while the warmth of the pretty creature and even the very roughness of the small three-cornered red tongue that licked her hand, as half-unconsciously she began to stroke the long soft fur, made her say suddenly:

"Who knows but it is the Will of the Creator! This mean-born thing may in the future be of use to the Light-of-the-World, the Observed-of-all-Observers," etc., etc., etc.

And her words were to come true, for, as you will see by and bye, Down was of great use to her little master. Nevertheless when, at the very next camping ground, a great big black golliwog of a dog with a gnawed end of rope still round his neck was seen calmly awaiting them at the door of the tent that was pitched for their reception, Head-nurse became tearful again and said that if Providence intended to send all the wild beasts of the field to look after Baby Akbar, there was no need for her; so she would give up her place.

But the little Prince himself was delighted. He plumped down on the hot sand beside the dog and hugged it, calling it "Dear Tumbu," and when the white cat jealously rubbed her back against his little fat person he hugged her too and called her "Darling Down."

"Hark to the Lord-of-the-Universe giving his creatures names!" said Foster-mother piously. So after that everybody

Flora Annie Steel

called the golliwog dog Tumbu, and the fluffy cat Down.

This was the beginning of a whole week on camel back; a very pleasant week too, though the minds of the elders were rather on the stretch concerning the fate of King Humayon and Queen Humeeda.

Still the sky was as blue as blue could be, the sun shone bright and the air was crisp with coming winter. Head-nurse spent most of her days dozing and mumbling long strings of titles in one pannier, while Down slept and purred on her lap. In the other pannier were Foster-mother and Baby Akbar. The little fellow did not sleep much, but spent most of his time craning over the pannier side to see everything there was to be seen. But what amused him most was to watch Tumbu, who would look up and bark and gambol for hours to attract his little master's attention. Whereat Down would become impatient and come over the camel's hump from the other pannier, rub her back against the little Prince and watch, too, with a sort of dignified contempt. It was the way of dogs to be loud and effusive, and gushing; but it didn't mean much. Tumbu, for instance, despite his display of affection, would leave his post to run after every wild thing he saw; and though he always came back to it, he was so helplessly breathless, with half a yard of red tongue hanging out, that he would have been little use had an enemy turned up and his protection been needed.

Cats were far wiser. They sat still and watched; so they were always ready.

And one evening Down watched to some purpose. Baby Akbar was asleep on some quilts and Down, as usual, lay keeping his feet warm, her eyes closed, purring away like a steaming kettle.

You would have sworn she was half asleep, but in a second there was one spring, something reared itself at her to strike, but her paws were too quick. One, two, three, came the blows swiftly like boxes on the ears, and there was a snake squirming and helpless in the dust. Old Faithful's armoured feet were on its head in a second and the danger was over.

"Truly a cat is a terrible thing," said Head-nurse in a twitter. "There is no fear in them. The reptile had not a chance."

But Down was back on her young master's feet, her eyes closed, purring away as if nothing had happened.

Tumbu was in favour, however, next evening, but for a different cause. He appeared with a great prickly porcupine held gingerly in his mouth and laid it before Baby Akbar.

"Ohi! Porcupine for supper!" cried Meroo, the cook boy, who knew what a delicacy it was; but Head-nurse shrieked, "Take it away quick—the Heir-to-Empire will prick himself with the quills and they are poisonous. Take it away at once, I say."

But alas! The Heir-to-Empire was wilful, like all Eastern Princelings, and he shrieked to match at the suggestion. So there arose such a hubbub, which was only calmed by Baby Akbar being allowed to do as he chose.

"Poor! Poor!" he said as his little hand touched the sharp prickles and no one found out, till Foster-mother came to put him to bed, that he really *did* scratch himself. There was quite a little runnel of blood on the palm; but Akbar, even when he was a baby, was proud. He knew how to bear discomfort and punishment when it was his own fault.

They were all rather merry that night, for they had roast

porcupine stuffed with pistachio nuts for supper. And afterward Roy sat by Baby Akbar's pile of quilts and sang him to sleep with this royal lullaby:

"Baby, Baby-ling,
You are always King;
Always wear a crown,
Though you tumble down;
Call each thing your own,
Find each lap a throne;
Dearest, sweetest King,
Baby! Baby-ling!"

When the child had fallen asleep Roy sat at the door of the tent and looked at the stars, which shone, as they do in the East, all colours, like jewels in the velvety sky. They seemed so far away, but not farther than he seemed to be from himself. For Roy's head had been dreadfully confused by that sunstroke in the desert. Only that morning something had seemed to come back to him in a flash, and he had so far forgotten he was only a page boy as to call the little Heir-to-Empire "Brother," but Head-nurse's cuff had brought him back to reality in double quick time. And as he sat there in the dark he saw a man creeping stealthily to the tent. He was on his feet in a moment challenging him.

"Hush!" whispered the newcomer, "I bring a message from King Humayon. I must see Foster-father at once."

The good man was already between the quilts, but he got up quickly, and when he had heard the message he sent for Head-nurse and Foster-mother and Old Faithful, for he felt that a most momentous decision had to be made. Yet the message was a very simple one. Those in charge of the child were to creep away that very night with the messenger, who would guide them in safety to King Humayon, who had found help and shelter in Persia.

Head-nurse and Foster-mother wept tears of joy at the glad news, and proposed at once that they should wrap the child in a blanket and start. But Foster-father was more wary.

"You come as a thief in the darkness," he said. "Where is your token from the king, that I may know who you are?"

But there was no token.

"Then the child stays where he is," asserted Foster-father boldly. "Am I not right oh! Faithful?"

"Assuredly my lord is right. Who knows but this man may be an emissary of those who would wile away the little lad from his uncle, Prince Askurry's protection. His other uncle, Kumran, is not so kind."

The messenger scowled at the old man. "As you please," he began blusteringly, "but those who disobey the King's order may find their lives forfeit."

"Mine is forfeit already to the child's service," replied Foster-father with spirit. "And without a token I stir not—Peace! woman," he added to Head-nurse, who would fain have sided with the messenger, "and go fetch the Heir-to-Empire's cap. That shall go as sign that he is his father's vassal, to do what he is told when the order comes accredited. So take that as my answer to those who sent you, sir messenger!"

So despite Head-nurse's protestations the man went off with nothing but the little gold-laced skull cap. And he had not to go far; only into a tent on the outskirts of the camp. For Foster-father's suspicions had been correct, and he had been sent to try and entice the child by some of Prince Kumran's partisans who, booted and spurred, and with a swift pacing camel for the child, were waiting eagerly for the return of their messenger.

Their faces fell as he flung the little cap upon the ground.

"The old fox is too wary," he said. "We must get at the child some other way."

One of the party took up the cap and fingered it, half idly. "He has a large-sized head for his years," he remarked; "if it be full of brains, hereafter he may do well."

CHAPTER VI

AT COURT

Of course, the messenger never returned from King Humayon with the token; but Foster-father was a good-natured man and did not boast of his wisdom to Head-nurse, who, however, remained wonderfully meek and silent until at the end of a fortnight's marching they saw, against the blue of the distant valley, the white domes of the town of Kandahar with the citadel rising above them. Then, with the chance of a court before her once more, she began chattering of ceremonials and titles and etiquettes.

"Praise be!" she shrilled in her high voice. "No more jiggett-ings and joggettings on camel back. I shall be on my own feet once more, and it shall not be my fault if His just dues are not given to the Great-in-Pomp—" etc., etc.

Foster-mother interrupted the string of titles. "So that they harm not the child," she said, clasping her charge tight. She was always thinking of his safety, always alarmed for danger; but he, young Turk that he was, struggled from her arms and pointed to the hills they were leaving behind them.

"Dadda, Amma 'way 'way mountains," he repeated once more; then added cheerfully, "Akka 'way, too."

Flora Annie Steel

"It is a prophecy!" said Old Faithful, overhearing the remark. "Sure his grand-dad Baber—on whom be peace—had the gift, and this babe may have inherited it."

"May have," echoed Head-nurse indignantly. "He has inherited it, and has much of his own besides. Mark my words! if this child live—which Heaven grant—he will be the King of Kings! Not two summers old and he talks as one of three."

"Aye!" assented Foster-mother, "but he does not walk yet."

Head-nurse sniffed. "Thou are a foolish soul, woman! Sure either the feet or the tongue must come first, and for my part I prefer the tongue. Any babe can walk!"

And Foster-mother was silent; it was true one could not have everything.

Their last camp was pitched just outside the city of Kandahar, so that Prince Askurry could make a regular triumphal entry the next morning and let everybody see with their own eyes that he had come back victorious, holding Baby Akbar as prisoner and hostage.

But this did not suit Head-nurse at all. She had no notion that her Heir-to-Empire should be stared at as a captive; so, though she started from camp humbly as ever on the baggage camel, no sooner had they passed through the arched gate of the city with Prince Askurry well ahead of them in the narrow streets, than out she whipped the Royal Umbrella which she had patched up with an old scarlet silk petticoat, and there was Baby Akbar under its shadow; and, having—young as he was—been taught to salute to a crowd, he began waving his little fat hand with much dignity, until the people who had come out to gape whispered among themselves and said:

"He looks every inch a king's son."

"And that is what he is," said a bold voice in the crowd; but though folk turned to see who spoke, there was no sign of the speaker. For loyal men had to hide their loyalty in those days. Still the populace were pleased with the little Prince's bearing, and many a hand was raised to welcome him.

Before they reached the frowning palace, indeed, where Prince Askurry kept a right royal court as Governor of Kandahar, Head-nurse's mind was full of the things she intended to insist upon for the honour and dignity of her small charge. Meanwhile she had to obey the order to take him at once into Princess Sultanam's apartments. Now Princess Sultanam was Prince Askurry's wife, and she had a boy of her own who was about three years older than Baby Akbar, and a little daughter who had just been born about a month before. So, as she lay among cushions at the farther end of the long room, with Prince Askurry, who had hurried to see his wife on his return, beside her, she looked suspiciously at the child which Head-nurse put down on the Persian carpet as soon as she came into the room; since though others might carry him to the upstarts at the farther end, *she* was not going to do so, when *they* were clearly bound to come humbly to the Heir-to-Empire and prostrate themselves before him!

So there stood Baby Akbar, fair and square, steadying himself by Head-nurse's petticoats, but for all that looking bold and big and brave.

Now Princess Sultanam was a kindly foolish woman at heart, much given to impulses, and the sight of the upstanding little boy made her think instantly what a fine man he would make, and that brought another thought which made her sit up delightedly and clap her hands.

Flora Annie Steel

"I have it, my lord!" she exclaimed, turning to Prince Askurry. "It is a grand idea! We will betroth our little Amina to this young master. That will settle everything and they will be the handsomest couple in the country!"

Now, strange as this may sound to my readers, Prince Askurry, who was accustomed to the Indian habit of settling that quite little boys and girls should marry each other when they grew up, could not help at once seeing that his wife's suggestion was not such a bad one. It would help him to keep a hold over the little Heir-to-Empire. If King Humayon returned it would make him more inclined to forgive, and if he did not, why! it would prevent cruel brother Kumran from stepping in and getting all, since as father-in-law to the young king he, Askurry, would be Regent.

Still, taken aback, he hummed and hawed.

"It would be a long time to wait until they are old enough to marry," he began.

"Long!" interrupted the lively Princess gaily. "All the longer for merriment and festivities. Thy daughter, my lord, is already beautiful, and I'll wager the boy will be a grown man ere we have time to turn round. So that is settled. Therefore come hither, oh nephew! Jallaluddin Mahomed Akbar, since that is thy long name, and kiss thy cousin Amina—Nurse! bring my sweeting hither. Now then, woman," she continued sharply, addressing Head-nurse, who stood petrified with astonishment and anger at the very idea of such scant ceremony. "If the boy cannot walk, carry him!"

Head-nurse could scarcely speak. To be called "Woman" by an upstart—for Prince Askurry had married Princess Sultanam for her beauty—was too much!

"The Feet-of-the-Most-Condescending-of-Majesties," she began pompously, "have not yet conferred happiness on the earth by treading it underfoot, neither—"

Here she broke off hurriedly, for at that very instant, as if in denial of her words, Baby Akbar gave a little crow of assent, let go her petticoats, and with outspread balancing arms, and legs very wide apart, launched himself boldly for his very first steps!

"*Bismillah!*" (Well done!) shrieked Foster-mother in delight.

"*Bismillah! Bismillah!*" echoed every one in the room, while all eyes full of smiles were on the stalwart young toddler as he lurched forward, his face one broad grin.

Princess Sultanam clapped her hands again. "Thy turban, my lord!" she cried in a flutter of amusement. "Thy turban, quick; as his father is not here 'tis thy place to prevent him falling of himself—thy turban—quick! quick!"

Prince Askurry, full of laughter, pulled off the soft turban he wore—it was all wound round and round to fit the head like a cap—and in obedience to the Indian custom, which always prevents a child from falling of itself in its first attempt at walking, flung it full at the little lad. It caught him between his outspread balancing arms and over he went on to the thick pile carpet.

Foster-mother was beside him in a second, eager to snatch him up and cover him with kisses; but Baby Akbar wriggled himself from her hold. He had set himself a task and he meant to do it.

"Go way!" he said with determination. "Tumbu down. Get up again."

So, calmly reaching round for the turban which lay beside him, which he evidently thought had tumbled down too, he clapped it on his head with both hands, rose to his feet and recommenced his forward lurch; a yard or two of the fringed turban, which had become unrolled, trailing behind him like a royal robe.

It was a quainter little figure than before, but nobody laughed now. They looked at each other, then at the child staggering along under the Prince's plumed turban, then at Prince Askurry himself standing bareheaded before his nephew.

It was an ill omen. And yet as Head-nurse said proudly when they got back to the rooms that had been given them in a frowning bastion of the palace, Baby Akbar had once more scored off his uncle.

Indeed, she was so cock-a-hoop about it that she stickled for this, and she stickled for that until the attendants, who were at first inclined to be civil, began to look askance, and Foster-father had to bid her hold her tongue.

"Wise folk leave steel traps alone," he said; "fiddling with them lets off the spring. Then—pouf!"

He shook his head significantly.

"Steel traps?" echoed Head-nurse sniffily, "who is talking of steel traps?"

"I am, woman!" replied Foster-father sternly. "I tell you this Kandahar is as a steel trap ready to snap on us at any moment."

Head-nurse was silent, even though he also had ventured to call her "woman"; but she was beginning to learn that nine times out of ten Foster-father was right.

CHAPTER VII

WINTER

The winter settled in early that year, and with the passes of the hills blocked by snow, the caravans of laden camels which, in addition to merchandise of all sorts, brought news from the world to the east and the world to the west of mountain-clipped Kandahar, ceased to come into the big bazaar. And the cold kept most people at home, or shivering beside the glowing braziers set outside the shops. It was not the season for active work, and so Prince Askurry let it slip by without really making up his mind what he was to do with Baby Akbar. Meanwhile the child could live in the bastion of the palace, and play with his little cousins. Whether he was to be betrothed to Baby Amina or not could be decided in the spring; this was the time for rest and home comfort without fear of any disturbing, since none could cross the passes in winter.

Princess Sultanam, however, to whom in her seclusion winter and summer were much alike, grew fond of the little lad, and never ceased to urge on her husband the wisdom of so treating Prince Akbar, that should King Humayon by good luck—and he *had* a knack of being lucky—find himself again with an army at his back, his hands would be tied from revenge on the Court at Kabul.

Flora Annie Steel

Now, Askurry was no fool; he saw that, for the present at any rate, until Humayon's fate was decided, it would be wiser to be kind; so he decided that when he held the New Year's assemblage he would present the little prince in due form to the chiefs and nobles.

Head-nurse was almost crazy with delight at the very idea. She and Foster-mother sent all their jewels to the goldsmith to be made up into suitable ornaments for Baby Akbar, and they ransacked the shops for odd scraps of brocade with which to make him the finest of fine state robes.

And on the eventful day they began the child's toilette early, pressing Roy the Rajput into service as tire-woman to hold the ointments, and scents, and what not, that they deemed necessary for the due dressing of a Prince.

So that it rather dashed their spirits when Foster-father came in with a sober face and the news that a man had come into the bazaar bringing bad tidings of the King and Queen. They had, he said, been lost in the snow; but whether this was true or not, who could tell?

"Then what is the use of worrying?" snapped Head-nurse, who was too much occupied in making her charge beautiful to think of other things. "Lo! Foster-father, evil is never lost on the road. It arrives sooner or later, so why watch for it at the door?"

"That is true," replied Foster-father, "but mark my words, all depends on good news. If that comes, the child is safe; if evil—then God help him!"

Roy, who, Baby Akbar being nearly dressed, was now holding the pot of lamp-black and oil with which Head-nurse, after the Indian custom, would put a finishing touch to her work by smearing a big black smut on the child's forehead, lest he should be too sweet and so attract an envious, evil eye, looked up at the words, his face full of light and remembrance.

"God does help true kingship," he said proudly. "Mother used to say so, and that is why she was never afraid—" He paused and the light in his face faded. "I—I don't remember any more," he added apologetically.

"Remembrance or no," snapped Head-nurse, "hold the pot straight, boy, or thou wilt spill it over the Mighty-in-Pomp, the Admired-of-the-World," etc.

But Foster-father looked at Old Faithful and laid his hand kindly on Roy's shoulder. "It matters not, Roy! It is there within thee, all the same. And 'twill come back some day, never fear. And I for one," he added aside to the old trooper, "should not wonder at much; for the lad's manners are ever above his present station."

Old Faithful shook his head wisely. "'Tis not the boy's manners, friend," he said, "but his breed. A man may compass manners for himself, but not that his father should have had them also."

By this time the black smear was on Baby Akbar's forehead, and despite the smudge, he looked a very fine little fellow indeed. So much so that quite a murmur of delighted admiration ran round the assemblage when Askurry appeared, leading him by the hand; for he had quickly learned to run about and was now quite steady on his legs.

"A chip of the old block," said an ancient mountain chief, who had known his grandfather Babar, and many others nodded assent. Then Prince Askurry began a set speech, little

Akbar seated on his knee the while.

It was a very clever, crafty speech, that could be taken two ways, and Prince Askurry was so much interested in it, and making sure that he was neither too disloyal or too loyal to his unfortunate brother, the King, that he did not notice what was passing on his knee until a sudden lack of attention on the part of his audience made him follow their eyes, and look down at the child upon his lap.

And then?

Then he sat dumbfounded, his face flushing to a dull, dark red, for he saw in a moment what the thing that had happened would mean to those others—the audience before him—the men he had summoned to listen to his half-hearted words.

Yet it was a very simple little thing. Baby Akbar, tired, doubtless, of his uncle's speechifying, had found amusement in a slender gold chain which hung round his uncle's neck; had traced it to a secret pocket in his inner waistcoat, and so had drawn out from its hiding place a golden signet ring, set with an engraved emerald. A toy indeed! So after playing with it for a bit the child had slipped it onto his little forefinger, which he held up the better to admire his new-found treasure. So it came to pass that as Askurry's smooth, oily voice went on and on, those who listened could see a little image sitting on his knee.

A dignified, gracious-looking image with forefinger held up in the attitude of kingly command; and on that forefinger—what?

The Signet of the King!

The Ring of Empire!

It was unmistakable! Askurry must have found it in his fugitive brother's tent. He must have concealed it. Uncertain what part he meant to play in the end, he must have worn it on his person until the child—the true Heir-to-Empire—

The chiefs looked at each other furtively. There was a pause. Then suddenly an old, thin voice—the voice of the old mountain chief, who remembered Babar the brave—rose on the silence.

"God save the Heir-to-Empire!"

It gave the lead, and from every side rose the cry:

"God save the Heir-to-Empire!"

Prince Askurry's face fell. He had not meant to rouse loyalty, but he was quick and clever, so he saw that it *had* been roused, and that now was not the time to try and stifle it. So his frown turned to a smile as he caught the child to him and rose, holding him in his arms.

"The rogue, my lords," he said lightly, "has forestalled me. I meant to place the ring upon his finger myself before you all, in token that he does in truth represent our King, but praise be to Heaven! he has saved me the task. Long live the Heir-to-Empire!"

But the nobles as they passed out of the assembly, and the people who heard the tale outside, said it was a strange happening that the innocent child should so claim his right. And cruel brother Kumran's party laid their heads together once more, and swore it was time to end Prince Askurry's foolish hesitation. They must get at the child somehow.

But by this time, if Prince Askurry had not quite made up his mind how he should treat Baby Akbar, he had quite settled that no one else—least of all cruel brother Kumran—should have anything to do with the child. So the little prince was carefully watched and guarded, rather to Foster-father's and Old Faithful's relief. Indeed, as time went on they almost forgot to watch themselves, being accustomed to see the sentry walking up and down before the entry to the narrow stairs that led up to the three rooms in the old bastion which were given them as lodgings. They were large, comfortable rooms, and the inner one was used by Foster-mother, Head-nurse and Baby Akbar, the outer one by the two men and the two boys, while the middle one, a great wide hall of a place, they used as a living room. It was lighter than the others, since it had slits of windows—without glass, of course—high up in the walls, and though these let the cold as well as the winter sunshine into the room, there was a roaring great fireplace, which kept the farther end of the hall nice and warm. And here on very frosty nights the women folk would drag their beds and sleep, while during the snowy days they would spread quilts on the floor, and Baby Akbar would have high jinks with Tumbu and Down, who were his constant playmates. Then, when he was tired, Roy would cradle his young master in his arms and sing to him. Not lullabies, for little Akbar's mind kept pace with his body, and every month saw him more and more of a boy and less and less of a baby.

"Tell me how Rajah Rasalu did this," or "Tell me how Rajah Rasalu did that," he would say; and so Roy's boyish voice would go over the old story of endless adventures, which has delighted so many Indian children for so many generations.

So time passed quite merrily until one night, when something dreadful happened. So dreadful that it will really require another chapter to describe it. But it was one night when Roy had been telling the little prince how "Rajah Rasalu's friends forsook him for fear." And as this is rather a nice story, it shall be told here.

"You know, great Kingly child," began Roy, "how Rajah Rasalu was born and how Rajah Rasalu set out into the world to seek for fortune, taking with him his dear horse, Baunwa-iraki, his parrot, Kilkila, who had lived with him since he was born, besides the Carpenter-lad and the Goldsmith-lad, who had sworn never to leave their young master. So he journeyed north to a lonely place, all set with sombre trees. And the night was dark, so he set a watch, and the goldsmith took the first, while the young prince slept by the Carpenter-lad, on a couch of clean, sweet leaves. And lest the heart of the prince should sink, they sang a cheering song:

> "'Cradled till now on softest down,
> Leaves are thy bed to-night;
> Yet grieve not thou at fortune's frown,
> Brave men heed not her slight.'"

"And while they slept and the goldsmith watched, a snake slid out from the trees. 'Now, who are you?' quoth the Goldsmith-lad, 'who come to disturb his rest?' 'Lo! I have killed all living things that have ventured within ten miles of this my place of rest,' it hissed, 'and now I will slay you, too!' So they fought and fought, but the Goldsmith-lad he killed the snake in the end. Then he hid the body under his shield, lest the others might be afraid, and he roused from his rest the Carpenter-lad, to take his share of the watch, while he, in his turn, on the clean, sweet leaves lay down beside the prince. And while they slept, and the Carpenter watched, a dragon slid from the trees. 'Now, who are you?' quoth the Carpenter-lad, 'who come to disturb his rest?' 'Lo! I have killed all living things for twenty miles round this place; and I'll kill you, too,' it roared, 'and crack your bones to eat.' So

Flora Annie Steel

they fought and fought and fought till he killed the dragon at last. Then he hid the body behind a bush lest the others should be afraid, and roused Rasalu from out his sleep to take his share of the watch; while he in turn by the Goldsmith-lad lay down to take his rest.

"And while they slept and Rasalu waked a THING slid out from the trees; an awful THING! No man could tell th' unspeakable horror of it. But Rasalu smiled in its face of dread, and laughed in, its horrible eyes. 'Pray, who are you to disturb our rest, and why do you dare to come?' 'Lo! I have killed all living things for twenty times twenty miles, and I will kill you, upstart boy, and crack your bones to dust.'"

"So they fought and fought and fought, and Rasalu drew his bow, and the arrow fled like the wind and pierced the Awful Horror through. Then it fled to a cave close by, with Rasalu at its heels. So they fought and fought and fought till the dawn showed clear in the sky, and the Awful Horror gave up with a groan and rolled on its side and died. Now, just as Rasalu wiped his sword the sleepers awoke from their sleep. 'See here!' said the Goldsmith-lad with pride, 'what I killed in my lonely watch.' 'Pooh! only a snake!' said the Carpenter-lad; 'see the dragon I have killed.' But Rasalu took them both by the hand and led them into the cave; but dead as it was, they shrieked with fear at the Awful Horror they saw. And they fell at Rasalu's feet and groaned and moaned and prayed and wept. 'Let us go! Oh, hero, we are but men. We dare not follow you now. It is nothing to you; it is death to us to follow and be your friends.'

"Then tears came into Rasalu's eyes, but he said no word of nay. 'Do as you will,' he said to them. '*I* will not bid you stay.

"'Aloes linger long before they flower,
Gracious rain too soon is overpast;

Youth and strength are with us but an hour,
All glad life must end in death at last.
But king reigns king without consent of courtier,
Rulers may rule, though none heed their command;
Heaven-crowned heads, stoop not, but rise the haughtier,
Alone and friendless in a strangers' land.'"

"So his friends forsook him and fled. But Rasalu went on his way."

CHAPTER VIII

DOWN'S STRATAGEM

Now the terrible thing that happened was one which Foster-father might have expected, but for two things.

One was the sentry who walked up and down all night long below the high second-story windows of the central room. He would be bound to see any attempt to gain an entrance through them, even if they were wide enough to admit the entry of a grown man, which they were not.

The other was the fact that he, Old Faithful, Meroo and Roy all slept in the outer room, into which the only door opened, so that any intruder would have to force an entrance over their bodies; for they slept with drawn swords beside them.

So as the days passed on Foster-father's vigilance—though he knew that cruel brother Kumran's agents were on the lookout for any opportunity of kidnapping the Heir-to-Empire—slackened somewhat, especially when the afternoons drew in, the fire in the big hall was made up, the quilts put down and Baby Akbar, surrounded by his admiring circle, listened to Roy's stories or tumbled about with his playmates, Tumbu, the dog, and Down, the cat.

One day, however, Down did not appear until little Akbar was having his supper, and then she came in a great hurry out of a small archway by the big fireplace, which led to a sort of cupboard in the masonry, where charcoal had been kept, gobbled up a plate of bread and milk, and hurried in again as if she had to catch a train.

"She has had kittens," said Foster-mother; "I wonder if they are white or black."

"Black!" sniffed Head-nurse. "What else could they be in that hole? Have a care, woman! or the Heir-to-Empire will be blacking himself, too. The archway is large enough for him to creep in, and Heaven only knows whither it might lead."

"That is true," replied Foster-mother, alarmed, as she distracted the child's attention.

But in a day or two his quick ear caught the sound of a feeble mewing inside the arch, and, of course, he wanted to know what it was. So he was told that kittens had to be kept quiet and that Down would be very vexed if her kitten was disturbed; but that by-and-bye she would doubtless bring it out for him to see, and then, of course, he could play with it. Now, Baby Akbar was always a reasonable little fellow, so he waited patiently; though every night when he went to bed and Down came out for her supper, his little mouth would go down and he would hold up his little hands and twiddle them round and say mournfully:

"Kitty not 'weady. Kitty not 'weady."

Now, one night there was a great festival in the palace, and the Heir-to-Empire had to go and pay his respects, after the Indian manner on feast days, to his aunt and uncle. Then, when he returned, they sent him, after Indian wont, trays full of fruit and sugar-toffee made in the shape of animals, and a few pieces of muslin and stuffs to make new dresses for the party. In addition to this there was a trayful of supper, which came afterward, when daylight had gone, with the Princess Sultanum's best compliments. At least so said the man who brought it; but he did not wait to be questioned, and disappeared so soon as Meroo had taken the tray from him.

But it was full of the most delicious dainties, including a bowl of sweet milk made with almonds and honey and rice meal for Baby Akbar.

Head-nurse, however, would not let him eat it. She was always afraid of the little lad being poisoned, so Meroo always cooked with his own hands everything the child ate. Therefore they gave it to Tumbu instead; for, having been brought up by shepherds, he loved milk, and he licked his lips after it and was soon sound asleep by the fire.

The lamb stewed with pistachio nuts and full of saffron looked, however, so delicious that after Meroo had tasted it and pronounced it quite safe, since all knew that saffron would not go with real poison, they set to work and finished the platter.

They were all as jolly as could be afterward, though the heat of the fire and their heavy supper made them sleepy; so Head-nurse, declaring it was far too cold in the inner room, dragged her bed and Foster-mother's close to the fire, the others retired to the outer room, and before long they were all snoring away quite happily.

For if the supper had not truly been poisoned, it had been drugged. Drugged with sleep-bringing drugs.

So, as the firelight flickered over the room faintly, it showed Head-nurse's face and Foster-mother's face and even Tumbu's black muzzle in a dead sleep that was almost unconsciousness. And in the outer room Foster-father snored, and even Roy's keen, hawk-face lay like one dead. Only Baby Akbar tossed and turned in his comfortable nest between his two nurses.

Save for this, due to Head-nurse's precaution in not allowing the Heir-to-Empire sweet milk for supper, all was as cruel brother Kumran's agents had planned when they had sent the pretended messenger from the palace with the platter of delicacies. Even the sentry below was sleeping sound after his share of kid curry.

Thus, those who were on the roof waiting until the moon had set and they could without fear of discovery lower the young lad, who was to steal Baby Akbar, down to the window (through which, being slender, the thief could slip easily), felt that their task was almost done.

But they reckoned without a great white fluff which after a time showed itself at the entry to the charcoal bunker, yawning and stretching and blinking its eyes. Head-nurse had been quite wrong in saying Down's kitten must be black in that hole! Its mother, anyhow, was beautifully white, perhaps because Down was a sensible cat and had only chosen the charcoal bunker because she had found a lot of old straw and a blanket tucked away in its farther corner. Besides, as she only had one kitten, she could spend all her time in licking it and cleaning it with her rough, red tongue, after the manner of cats. Anyhow, there it lay, right out of reach of any one, a little bundle of white fluff, and Down was just beginning to feel that there were other things in the world besides kittens. For instance, was that scratching on the roof, think you, a mouse? If so—? She passed to the fire.

It was warm and nice; just the very place for a kitten's first look at the world, and there were no troublesome people about; not but what she was anxious to show her kitten to Baby Akbar. But who knew if horrid Head-nurse might not try to catch it? But Head-nurse was asleep. Down whisked her tail, disappeared through the archway, and reappeared again gingerly, carrying the kitten in her mouth. It sprawled in the firelight and mewed piteously. And there was that scratching on the roof again ... really, kittens were a bore when one wanted to mouse....

So far it is easy to follow Down's thoughts. What came next is more difficult. No one can say whether the cat had *really* any notion that danger to her young master was abroad, or whether she only wanted to show him her kitten, or whether she wanted it taken care of—for Persian cats, if they kill a rat at night, have often been known to jump on their master's bed and insist on his taking custody of their prize lest it should somehow come to life again if they left it alone— only this was certain, Baby Akbar woke with a rough, red tongue licking his nose, and there, on the quilt, was Down beside the fluffiest, darlingest little kitten that ever was!

He made a grab at it with his little fat hands. Whether this frightened its anxious mother or whether Down really had a purpose in view, who can say? Only this is sure: she was off the bed in a second, Miss Kitten in her mouth. A minute afterward Baby Akbar was off it also with a little crow of delight. But the drugged nurses did not stir; they were away in the Land of Dreams. And hark! what was that curious noise outside the window, as if something was slipping down the wall? Perhaps it was *that* that frightened Down once more; for just as Baby Akbar's hand reached out to lay hold of the kitten, which she had set down by the fire, Down snatched it up again and was off with it back to the charcoal bunker, with Baby Akbar after her, his face full of solemn resolve. He meant to play with that kitty.

And play with her he did. At least, after he disappeared down the archway by the fireplace he did not come out again. Only Down reappeared and seated herself at the entrance, her ears cocked, her eyes fixed on the window.

For something very funny had happened there, which, though the flicker of the fire had died down, she could see with her cat's eyes.

A lad had slipped in, carrying the end of a rope, to which was attached a network bag. And now, since it was dark, he was striking a light. A feeble little glimmer, but sufficient to show the two sleeping nurses and the comfy little nest of quilts between them. But it was empty!

The boy seemed puzzled, and went into the inner room, only to return without what he sought. Then he stole into the outer room, but came back softly with a puzzled look on his face. Then he began to peer about him on the floor, and in the corners, holding the feeble light in front of him. Whereupon Down, apparently to satisfy herself that her kitten really was safe in the corner of the charcoal bunker where she had left it, retreated for a moment, so that as the searcher came round he saw nothing but the low, round arch. The next he gave a stifled yell, for something white that was all claws leaped right in his face, over he went and out went his light.

"I look no more," he said, shivering as, after five minutes' hasty retreat, he stood on the roof among those who had sent him down. "Let some one else go; but I tell you the child is not there."

But one of the crafty, cruel men had sharp wits. "Could he have crept into the charcoal bunker?" he suggested, and the faces round him lit up. But the lad's remained sullen, as he wiped the blood from Down's scratches.

"Mayhap," he said. "*But I go not near that cat again!*"

So, as no one else was small enough to slip through the narrow slits of windows, the conspirators could only curse their bad luck.

Thus it came to pass that the hours passed by without further attempt at baby-theft, while Foster-father snored and Head-nurse dreamed the most heavenly dreams of wonderful court ceremonials, and all the others were wrapped in the profoundest slumbers.

But they all woke at last, and once more there was the most terrible hullabaloo until Foster-mother recollected the kitten in the charcoal bunker. Whereupon every one in turn flattened themselves on the floor and reached in, and Roy actually got his head and one shoulder in; but no one could feel anything or find out how big it was or anything about it. Whereupon the two women began mutual recriminations and the men stood helpless, when suddenly Down appeared with the kitten in her mouth, and Baby Akbar, who had evidently been comfortably asleep on the blanket amid the straw, came crawling after his new pet.

"So far so good!" said Foster-father, who, noticing a fallen piece of mortar at the window-sill, had been carefully examining certain signs and scratches both without and within, "but if I be not much mistaken, some one hath been through here this night. And that we were all drugged ye must know if the inside of your mouths be like mine! So we have to thank Heaven and the cat for an escape!"

And so they had, though it was a sore trial once more to the women to have nothing but guesswork to go upon.

"I wish I knew," murmured poor Foster-mother mournfully, as she watched Baby Akbar, and Down, and the kitten, and Tumbu, all playing together before the fire.

But once more Baby Akbar was silent, and Down told nobody—unless it was Tumbu. Perhaps he *did* know, because he allowed Down's kitten to play with his tail!

Flora Annie Steel

CHAPTER IX

SPRING

Winter passed to spring and spring to early summer, and yet no certain news came of King Humayon or Queen Humeeda. Foster-father almost gave up hope, yet he said little, though he took counsel with Old Faithful, and he in his turn consulted the old mountain chief, who at the assemblage had been the first to cry, "Long live the Heir-to-Empire."

But the old man shook his head. The times were new, he said; very few people remembered, as he did, the old ways, the old Kings. But for the sake of Babar the brave they might always count on his sword and the sabres of fifty or more of his followers. So, if the worst came to the worst, they were welcome to an asylum in his eagle's eyrie of a fortress, where at any rate they could all die together fighting for the King; and what more did any brave man want?

This was not much consolation to Foster-father, who felt that there was nothing to be done, save by every means in his power, to curry favour with the Princess Sultanum.

But, indeed, the little Heir-to-Empire made himself friends wherever he went; they could not help liking the frank little fellow who spoke to them so freely, with a certain grave dignity of his own. For by the time the peach gardens around Kandahar lay like clouds of pink and white about the old domed city, little Prince Akbar was in looks and ways a child of three or even four; so big and strong was he. He spoke perfectly in his childish way, with great emphasis and a curious, soft burr over his r's and h's. And he actually tried to wrestle with his cousin Ibrahim, who was, however, rather a puny boy, despite the fact that he was three years older than the little Heir-to-Empire.

But with Roy as playmate Akbar began all sorts of games. There was a high, walled peach garden not far from the bastion, where the little Prince used to be allowed to go; and there, during the long sunny hours, the Rajput lad, to whom such things were all curiously familiar, taught the child how to ride on Tumbu's back, and how to hold a spear. Aye! and to take a tent peg, too; the peg being only a soft carrot stuck in the earth! But the great game was shooting with a bow and arrow, and in this, before spring passed to summer, the pupil was a match with his teacher except in strength; for, from the very beginning, Akbar showed himself steady and straight as a shot; so it is no wonder he grew up to be the finest marksman in India. But it would take too long to tell all the games they played, all the manly sports which the little prince learned without any difficulty. There was a shallow marble tank in the middle of the garden, where he took to the water like a duck, and would lie on his back and kick and shout with laughter as the tank got rough with waves, till Foster-mother would beg him not to drown, as the water splashed over him high in the air.

But Foster-father always reproved her for her fears. "Leave the lad to learn King's ways," he said, "and thank Heaven the Rajput foundling is here to teach him. Think you *I* could tumble head over heels in air or water or ride bareback standing on one leg?"

Flora Annie Steel

"No, indeed!" would reply Head-nurse, who stifled her terrors from a sense of duty, "none, seeing thy figure, friend, would ask so much of thee."

Then, when Akbar grew tired, Roy would sit leaning his back against a peach tree so as to make a soft pillow for his little master, and Akbar would lean against him and listen to endless stories while the soft fresh breeze stole over the garden wall, and sent showers of pink peach petals on both the boys. And sometimes the little Prince, outwearied, would fall asleep, and then Roy would sit still as a mouse, gently flicking away with the end of his muslin turban the blossoms that fell on the little sleeper's face. But his thoughts would be busy, wondering above other things why it was that, do what he would, he could not help when they were alone at play sometimes calling the Heir-to-Empire "little brother." It was dreadfully wrong of him, of course, and Head-nurse would rightly cuff his ears if she overheard it!

Then Akbar would wake and call imperiously for some favourite story, and as often as not it would be the tale of "How Rajah Rasalu swung the Seventy Maidens."

And Roy would reply submissively: "It is ordered, High-ness!" and begin:

"Now Rajah Rasalu, soft heart and strong, heard a pitiful voice as he rode along. 'Oh traveller! traveller! turn aside, and help God's creature,' it moaned and cried. So the Prince turned straight and saw that a fire had caught a bush, blazing higher and higher, while a tiny cricket lay gasping for breath, half-scorched, half-choked, and nigh to its death. Then Rajah Rasalu, soft hearted and stout, put his hand in the fire and snatched it out! And the cricket drew forth a feeler and said: 'Take this, my preserver, 'twill bring you aid; should *any* thing *ever* prove troublesome, burn *this* in the fire and *I* will come.' Then Rasalu laughed with a great big laugh, 'I thank you, weakling! But none of your chaff! *You* couldn't help *me* I'll go bail.' So he rode on careless o'er hill and dale, a glittering knight in his shining mail, till he came to the city of King Surkap, whom he'd sworn to kill with his sword so sharp. Now as he rode through a garden gay, Seventy Maidens barred the way; Seventy Maidens young and fair, with flowers decking their golden hair. Seventy daughters of the king, come out to play and laugh and swing and jibe at the stripling who'd sworn to slay their father, the mightiest king of this day. But the youngest maid had a heart of gold, and when she saw Rasalu so bold, and strong and handsome riding to death, on his horse Iraki, she caught her breath, and whispered to him as he passed her way:

> "'Fair prince on thy charger so gray,
> Turn thee back, turn thee back.
> If thou lowerest thy lance for the fray,
> Thy head will be forfeit to-day.
> Dost love life? then, stranger! I pray
> Turn thee back—turn thee back.'"

"But Rasalu smiled in the maiden's face, and drew his rein for an instant's space, while he gave her answer with courtly grace: 'Fair maiden, I come from afar, sworn conqueror in love and in war. Thy father my coming will rue, for his head in four pieces I'll hew. Then forth as a bridegroom I'll ride with you, little maid, as my bride.'"

"Now at these words, and his face so kind, and strong, and brave, the maiden's mind fluttered, the blood through her heartstrings whirled, she felt she could follow him through the world; but her sixty-nine sisters were jealous and cried: 'Not so fast, young man! If *she* be your bride, *you* be our younger brother, beside! So do our bidding or go on your way.' 'Fair sisters,' quoth he, 'let me hear your say!' Now the sisters vowed he should not succeed, so they took a whole hundred-weight of seed, as fine as the hundred-weight of sand they mixed it with, then gave command: 'If you wish to marry our sister, sir, take the seed from the sand without demur.'"

"Then Rajah Rasalu stood aghast; but he thought of the cricket's gift at last, and taking it out of his pocket thrust it into the fire, and a cloud as dust showed in the sky and the distant whirr of thousands of wings caused the air to stir, as, dark'ning the day like a fun'ral pall, a flight of crickets appeared at the call. 'What is our task?' asked his friend with a laugh; 'only *that*? I've brought too many by half!' So they set to work with a will indeed, till the sand lay separate from the seed, and sixty-nine maidens pouted and frowned as they wondered *what* new task could be found, to puzzle Rasalu and keep him there a slave to the wishes of maidens fair. 'Now swing us all, sir, one by one, when we grow tired your task is done!'—they laughed in their sleeve, for they knew right well, that when they'd be tired, none could tell!

"But Rasalu laughed: 'What! seventy girls—for my little bride is the pearl of pearls—and only one man to swing the lot! Shall I spend my life in such silly rot? No! into one swing the seventy go; I'll fasten the rope to my mighty bow, and shoot an arrow for all I know, so in with you, girls, sit all in a row, and don't be frightened, my little dears, I'll swing till you're tired, so have no fears.'"

"Then the seventy clambered into one swing—so merry, so careless, their voices ring. And Rasalu stood in his shining array, as merry and careless as happy as they. He fastened the ropes to his mighty bow, and bent till it would no further go; then with a twang he loosed the string, and like an arrow the laden swing with its burden of seventy maidens fair, shot like an arrow into the air. Merry and careless with laugh and smile, up in the sky for many a mile; like a soaring bird in the distant blue, while merry and careless, and tall and true, Rasalu waited upon the plain, till the swing swung back to its place again. Then he out with his sword and laughed anew, 'Ye have had a fine ride, ye giggling crew; enough and to spare, so out with you there!' Then he severed the ropes with one mighty sweep, and the seventy maidens fell in a heap; and some were broken and some were bruised, and the only one that was not ill-used was the youngest maid, for she did not drop till the very last, so she fell on top!"

And here Prince Akbar used always to laugh gravely and say: "Glad she didn't tumble down *really*, for she was a nice little girl."

One day when the peach blossoms had all floated away, leaving in their place grey-green fluffy ovals that by-and-bye would be luscious ripe fruits, Foster-father arrived in a great state of excitement just as Rasalu had finished swinging his Seventy Maidens.

"News, news!" he cried; "real news at last; and thank Heaven they are good! My master, the King, has not only secured shelter, but help, and hath written to his brother, Prince Askurry, advising him not to listen to ill advice, but to give in his allegiance at once, when all shall be forgotten. In token of which clemency he is sending to his still-dearly-beloved brother, Her Royal Highness the Princess Bakshee Bani Begum, that she may be a companion to her half-brother, the Heir-to-Empire."

Prince Akbar, who was leaning on Roy's breast, suddenly sat up. "Is that my sister?" he asked eagerly, "is she a nice little girl like Rasalu's bride?"

Head-nurse laughed. "Nice enough I'll warrant, though I

never saw her; she has been since she was born, six years past, with her mother's people; but so long as they send no fine ladies of nurses with her she is welcome."

Little Prince Akbar stood up and stretched himself, and looked at Head-nurse critically.

"Akka will welcome her, and Akka will tell you to be her nurse, and Akka will swing her a great big swing."

So far as he was concerned *that* settled the question; but up at the Court there were endless questionings of heart. Prince Askurry was, as ever, in two minds as to what he should do. Cruel brother Kumran, who was Governor at Kabul, pressed his advice to stand firm, to send the child to him, to let him show King Humayon that paid Persian troops could not stand up against Indian ones. But Princess Sultanum had really become fond of the little Heir-to-Empire, and felt sure that if they only played their cards carefully the king, out of gratitude, would consent to a betrothal between his son and her little daughter Amina. And in the end the wife's counsel prevailed. So a better lodgment was found for the royal children in an old palace surrounded by a lovely garden, and here, just as the roses were beginning to bloom, little Prince Akbar, dressed in his best, stood awaiting his sister's arrival. He had insisted on having, like Rajah Rasalu, a coat of mail; so Foster-mother had made him a tight-fitting corselet of silver tissue, in which he looked very fine indeed, as he stood brandishing a wooden sword covered with tin foil.

But when the red and gold bedecked camel did finally come up the marble-paved pathway with silent soft elastic swing, little Akbar forgot all about the part he was playing, and when he saw his sister, just ran up to her and hugged her tight, and said breathlessly: "Ah! you are a nice little girl!"

And a very nice little girl she was! Very small for her age, with a little oval delicate face, big hazel eyes, and brownish hair all plaited in tiny, tiny little plaits on her forehead.

And she was dressed just like a grown-up, with little ear-rings and wristlets and anklets and necklaces and rings, with the dearest, daintiest of flimsey gauze veils set with little silver stars wound all about her! Never, said Head-nurse, had been such a darling little marionette, and when the small person fell gracefully at her brother's feet and begged his favour in a little piping voice, that stern believer in court etiquette was perfectly enchanted.

"It will be a real boon to the First-Gentleman-of-the-World, the Courtly-one-of-Courts, etc., etc., to have the society of his equals," she said with a darkling look at Princess Sultanum's Head-nurse, who had brought Prince Ibrahim and Baby Amina to welcome their cousin.

But, after all, Bakshee Bani Begum did not turn out so demure as she looked! Indeed, when Head-nurse was not by, she was a regular tomboy; and after a whole morning spent in most lady-like fashion either playing with her dolls, or stringing beads, while Down, the cat, on her lap blinked and purred and stared out on the world with her big blue eyes and her little white feet tucked well inside, she would, when the women retired to get ready the mid-day meal, spring up like a squirrel, scattering beads and cats as if they were of no account! Then the garden would re-echo to children's laughter.

And she would let Mirak, as she elected to call her brother, swing her for hours, but she obstinately refused to tumble down!

"But, Bija," expostulated the little lad, "the princess did

Flora Annie Steel

tumble down in the story."

"I am not a princess *in a story*," said Bija calmly, "I am Her Royal Highness Princess Bakshee Bani Begum."

CHAPTER X

THE NIGHT OF RECORD

So the summer days passed and winter set in once more. Though more satisfied, Foster-father felt still that safety depended on King Humayon's success or failure.

So, whenever one of the long files of camels tied together in a string, head-and-tail, showed on the hill road above Kandahar, he was off to the halting-place outside the city to see what news it had collected in its march from Hindustan; for caravans in those days were the postmen.

And sometimes he heard one thing, and sometimes another, but as often as not he returned as he went, without any remedy but patience.

"Anyhow the child grows in stature and strength," Head-nurse would say, "and our present lodging is better than our last!"

Which was true; for the old house of three stories which they now inhabited was full of little rooms leading one out of the other like a rabbit-warren. And if there was no furniture in them, so much the better for the children's games of "I espy" and "Touch who Touch can."

Flora Annie Steel

For Bija and Mirak played such games with infinite zest. As Head-nurse had foretold, the coming of his little sister had been an immense gain to the Heir-to-Empire; not only in manners, but also in his outlook upon life. For Princess Bakshee Bani Begum was a very determined small person, who did not in the least see why the elder sister of a boy should give way to him in all things, simply because he was Heir-to-Empire.

"I won't have it, Mirak," she would say with a stamp of her little foot; "you shall not break my doll's head just because you want to."

So Prince Akbar, who was full of sound common sense, began to think she had reason on her side; and this was of great advantage to him, for with Head-nurse, and Foster-mother and the others, he stood a great chance of being spoiled.

And after a time he became quite devoted to the prim little maid, who, for all her primness in general, could be as wild as a hawk on occasion.

And out of that arose an incident which, unfortunately, turned Princess Sultanum against the little lad and so endangered his safety. It came about in this way. Prince Askurry's son Yakoob was, as has been said, three years older than Akbar, a lanky, rather weedy lad-ling of nearly six. Now Prince Askurry was himself a noted wrestler, and was determined his son should be one also. So he had the boy carefully taught, and set a good deal of store by the quickness of the little fellow in learning the grips, and how to trip up an adversary. On high days and holidays, indeed, Prince Askurry and his wife used often to amuse themselves by seeing the discomfiture of other less experienced children who were set up to compete with the young wrestler. Baby

Akbar had been one of these, and being so much younger, he had always gone down before Yakoob's skill; but he had always taken his overthrow in good part, though Head-nurse had felt as if she could not keep her fingers off the victor. It was not fair, she would say afterwards, to match a baby of two with a child of six, and then she would try to hug the vanquished Heir-to-Empire and cover him with kisses; but Akbar, always independent, resented this. "Akbar tumble *him* down some day," he would say philosophically; and indeed there seemed every chance of it, for, mere baby as he was, there was more promise of future strength in his little finger than in Yakoob's whole body.

Now, as winter came on, the children were driven indoors for their play, and Old Faithful at their earnest request, rigged up a swing in a large empty room in the palace, and here Princess Bija would be swung like the Seventy Maidens, until Prince Akbar wearied of swinging her; and knowing that nothing would induce his elder sister to tumble down like the princesses in the story, would say quite plaintively:

"Please, Bija, get down; I'm tired of being Rasalu," when the little maid would descend gracefully and they would play at something else.

But one day, just after the New Year, Prince Yakoob came to spend the day with his cousins, and the children fell to acting the adventures of Rajah Rasalu; Yakoob, as the guest, playing the hero's part.

They got through several of them quite successfully, Princess Bija making a spirited carpenter's lad and killing his dragon with great vigour, while the Heir-to-Empire, disguising his deep baby voice in a high squeak, doubled the parts of the seventy-nine maidens and the cricket. So all went merry as a marriage bell until Rasalu had to order the giggling crew out of the swing.

Then, of course, Bija refused; whereupon Yakoob, a spoiled boy, cast aside the tinsel-covered wooden sword, and whipped out from his belt a toy dagger his father had given him that morning. It was not very sharp, but very little cuts a taut rope, and one furious slash severed some of the strands, the weight of the two children did the rest, and there they were both on the marble floor!

And unfortunately the "pearl of pearls," Rajah Rasalu's bride, did *not* fall on top. She fell underneath the Heir-to-Empire, and the Heir-to-Empire was heavy! So there was her poor little lip all cut and her pretty little nose all bleeding. Then *two* Head-nurses rushed in, and *two* Foster-mothers, and ever so many pairs of nursery attendants, each taking the part of their respective nurslings, and there was a terrible to-do, for, of course, one Head-nurse said it was the fault of the other Head-nurse, and so on. In fact peace did not return until the party separated and the offender, Prince Yakoob, was being joggetted back to his mother by his excited attendants, while Princess Bija was having her swollen nose soothed by cold water. She did not cry much, but she was terribly indignant with every one, including her brother.

He couldn't have prevented his cousin from cutting the rope, of course, but he might have made his cousin's nose bleed also! If she hadn't been otherwise occupied she could have done it herself; she was quite sure she could; or at any rate have done something quite as disagreeable!

She looked very fierce as she spoke, while Akbar listened with grieved attention. In fact, what Bija would have done, had Head-nurse not had her in her arms cossetting her, became quite a subject of conversation between the two children, Bija sitting demurely threading beads and inventing new methods of just punishment, and the Heir-to-Empire lolling on the floor pretending to sharpen his tinfoil sword, and interposing objections such as, "But you couldn't do *that*, Bija, you're not *strong* enough," or "*That* wouldn't be fair, Bija, for he only hurt you a little, you know." For Akbar was born with a sense of fair-play and justice which never forsook him, because he always gave *it* fair play.

So the idea of somehow getting the better of Yakoob became a fixed one in the little lad's mind until an opportunity for action came to him.

It was about a month afterwards, on the "Festival of Record"; that is to say, the day when good Mohammedans pray for guidance during the coming year, and believe that God's Angel, accompanied by the spirits of their dead ancestors, appears on earth to judge the record of the past year, and write on the forehead of each man and woman and child what reward or punishment is deserved in the next. In the evening, thousands of little lamps are lit, so that there shall be no darkness anywhere, but all things shall be made manifest, and when the little platters of sweets and food are set out lest any of the spirits, who come to plead for their descendants, should feel hungry, it is a very solemn affair; but the day is generally spent in amusement.

So Princess Sultanum arranged an entertainment, and, as usual, there was to be a bout of wrestling between her son and some little companions, amongst them the Heir-to-Empire. Head-nurse was furious, of course. The show was invented, she declared, to disgrace the Mighty-in-Pomp, the Pole-star of the Universe, etc., etc.

Akbar himself took it very complacently and allowed himself to be undressed and oiled all over, so as to make a grip very hard; for these are the Indian customs. And a very sturdy specimen he looked as he stood up and crossed his arms and then slapped himself with resounding slaps before crossing them again; also after Indian fashion, for so much he had learned of wrestling.

Then the signal was given, and Yakoob, as was his wont, began, in imitation of grown-up wrestlers, to steal an advance on his adversary.

But Akbar would none of that. Whether, watching real wrestling, he had noticed the method of attack he employed, or whether Roy had taught him, or whether he got it out of his own head, does not matter; but the little fellow rushed forward furiously and charging like a butting ram, caught his cousin full in the stomach, then making a snatch at his ankle tripped him up. So there in a second was Yakoob on his back, and Akbar, breathless but triumphant, on top of him.

"Now *you've* tumbled down," remarked the Heir-to-Empire suavely, as, astride his cousin's prostrate body, he paused for breath ere getting up.

Of course, some people said it wasn't fair; but others admitted that though not the *polite* style of wrestling, such a method was strictly within the rules. All, however, admired the big, bold, strong little Heir-to-Empire; all but his aunt and uncle; and the former bid Head-nurse take away her young savage at once, while the latter's crafty face, uneasy before, settled into a scowl.

But Head-nurse could hardly contain her joy, even when Foster-father shook his wise old head and said he would not have had it happen for all the wealth of the world, for of late, if he were not much mistaken, things had been shaping ill for his young master, and that very morning a secret messenger had come in from Kabul. What it might portend who could say; but it was bad fortune the child should lose favour at Court to such slight purpose.

"Slight, indeed!" sniffed Head-nurse. "Is it not something to have shown that woman that her brat cannot stand up before true Kingship?"

"I would it were so, woman," replied Foster-father, "but a child under three with but two old men and two boys for protection cannot show much fight."

Head-nurse tossed her head. "So we women are not to count—" she began; but Baby Akbar had been listening seriously and now put in with his deep childish voice, and a wise little shake of the head:

"And there's Tumbu and Down, too; they can bite and scratch beautifully for me when they like."

Whereupon Foster-mother caught him up, and wept, and swore that Heaven must and would protect such a heart's darling.

Perhaps it was this conversation which put the idea of getting help into the children's heads, but after a time it was evident they had some plan between them, for after watching the women light hundreds of little lamps, and set out a quantity of tiny platters full of sweets, they stole off by themselves to an empty room which was almost dark and began to whisper.

"I think it had better be grand-dad," said the Heir-to-Empire gravely, "'cos my father isn't dead yet, and they must be deaders, you know, if they are *really* to help."

"And we'll take the little summer room at the very top of the house, Mirak, so's we'll be able to stop him on his way down, 'case any one else has got a platter for him," said Bija the practical. "Now, Mirak, I'll fetch the sweets if you'll get some lamps. They won't be missed, you know, if we take them betwixt and between."

After that there was much secret hurrying up and down stairs and secret gurglings of delight as the preparations advanced.

"Oh, Mirak! Won't it be lovely? He's sure to come in when he sees it!" said the little girl, clasping her hands. "And Old Faithful was saying that Grand-dad Babar was as good as twenty other men in a fight, so *then* you'll be quite safe."

But Mirak's face was solemn. "If Grand-dad doesn't know it's for him he won't come in, and he won't eat the sweets either. It's greedy to eat sweets as doesn't belong to you, and *he* wasn't greedy. Old Faithful says he wasn't. He was a real King."

"Don't you think he might be greedy just to help you?" suggested Bija mournfully; but after thinking a little she clapped her hands. "I have it, Mirak! If his name was on it that would do! I think I could write 'Ba-ba.' It's only the two first letters, you see, and I know *them*; and you could prick yourself for some blood to write with, and I could use my little finger as a pen. It's very, very tiddly wee."

It was, indeed! and Mirak sat large-eyed in admiration of his sister's ingenuity, while she, mistress of the situation, did this and that until even she was satisfied. And really the little arched and domed cupola set in Eastern fashion on the roof, looked quite pretty with the little glittering lights in a square on the white marble floor, and the platter of sweets placed in the middle of the square, whereon in smeared red letters showed this:

"And now, Mirak!" chattered Bija, "we'll go down and go to bed like good boys and girls, and then when the others are saying their prayers and going to sleep we can come up again and sleep here."

"Won't it be very cold, Bija?" asked Mirak, whose little nose was half frost-bitten already, for a cold wind was blowing off the snow hills.

"We will bring quilts," said the little lady with a superior air.

So, about an hour afterwards, after the children had been put to bed and their elders had begun the serious work of watching and waiting and dozing through the night, two little figures, well wrapped up in quilted cotton gowns and draging quilted cotton blankets behind them, stole up the stairs to the roof of the house.

"I'm going to ask God to let him come," said Baby Akbar solemnly. So they both touched the cold marble floor with their warm little foreheads and said:

"Please Great God! Let our grand-dad Babar come and take care of us, and be kind to us, and not let the Angel write nasty things on our foreheads for this next year!"

Then they cuddled themselves closely together in the blankets and were soon fast asleep.

So fast asleep that even when, after the short hullaballoo which followed on the discovery that they were not in their beds, they were traced to the roof, they did not thoroughly wake up, but were carried down again without knowing much about it.

"Shall I blow out the lights?" asked Roy, as Head-nurse

Flora Annie Steel

prepared to descend also.

Head-nurse looked round to Foster-father for his opinion.

"No!" he said shortly, "leave them! The children have asked some one to eat those sweets. Let be! They may want all the help they can get."

So all the night long the little lamps twinkled and twinkled.

But when morning came there was not a sweet left!

"It must have been the rats," said Meroo, who, as cook, had gone up to see what he could save. "I saw the tail of one disappearing."

But Foster-father said swiftly: "I would it were some other helper, for the time has come for help. Prince Askurry hath sent to say we start for Kabul and cruel brother Kumran at noon to-day!"

CHAPTER XI

A WINTER MARCH

It was only too true! The escort which was to see them on the road was already occupying the garden, the horses champing their bits and fretting because the long branches of the roses at which they snatched held nothing but thorns.

Prince Akbar, indeed, was too much interested in watching them and wondering if they were very hungry to take much heed of anything else, but Princess Bakshee Bani Begum, who was a very practical little person, at once began to pack up her favourite doll.

"You had better choose out some toy, Mirak," said she, "or you will be wanting to play with mine, and I won't let you."

But Mirak was busy with the horses.

"I sha'n't want anything but my sword," he replied valiantly. "I'm a big boy now, and I'm going to play with real things." Then he turned to one of the troopers with a quaint air of authority. "Your horse is too thin. When I am King I shall see that my men give their horses enough to eat."

Foster-father, who overheard the child, paused in the hasty

Flora Annie Steel

arrangements he was making to look at the little Heir-to-Empire and put up a prayer that the fates might let him be King; but the future looked black indeed. The road to Kabul must still be blocked with snow, even if more did not fall by the way. A likely happening, with the bitter north wind and the dull lowering sky. And if the young child escaped the danger of extreme cold and extreme hardship, what might not be before him in Kabul itself?

Better, it might have been, for those in charge of him, to have risked all, taken refuge with the old mountain chief, and died like brave men. There was but one comfort in the whole affair. Prince Askurry must know that Humayon or his friends were close at hand, or he would not be in such a desperate hurry to send away the Heir-to-Empire.

And this, indeed, was the truth. The fear of a rescue was so real and immediate that Prince Askurry had had to make his decision in a minute. So there was scarcely any time for preparation, and by noon the party had started for the three hundred and odd miles of mountainous country that lay between them and Kabul. Only the children's faces were cheerful; even Roy's showed grave and anxious.

They rode fast and far till dusk fell, when they had covered full twenty miles. For the last few, both the women, who were mounted behind troopers, had almost been dropping with fatigue, but the captain of the escort was under orders to go as far as possible that night, so he pushed on to reach a place called Robat. Here they were all unceremoniously bundled into one large room, and by the steady tramp through the night of a sentry outside, Foster-father judged they were complete prisoners. Luckily they were given plenty of fuel to replenish the fire that roared in the wide chimney, so the elders squatted round it and dozed, holding the children in their laps. They slept as soundly as if they had been in their beds, and so did Tumbu and Down, who had both insisted on being of the party; the latter having quite calmly taken her place on Horse-chestnut's broad wavy back on the wide cushion of felt which Foster-father used as a saddle-cloth. She had left her kitten behind her as it was now quite a big tom-cat, and able to take care of itself.

In a way, both Tumbu and Down had already been of service to their young master, for the troopers of the Escort had been amused by the golliwog's gambols, and had admired Down's dignity, so they were more inclined to treat the whole party in kindly fashion. Indeed, next morning, the Captain of the Escort, whose anxiety about a rescue had, perhaps, been lessened by the uneventful night, was much less strict in his orders, and took Prince Akbar on his own saddle and let him hold the reins.

"He is a brave, bold lad," he said to Foster-father; "were he to live, he would make a good King." Then he frowned, his mouth hardened and Foster-father, watching him, augured ill for the safety of the Heir-to-Empire. For the time, however, all went well, though Foster-father remarked that they kept off the direct track as much as possible; no doubt to avoid pursuit. And at Ghuznee, where they halted the second night, the Captain of the Escort sent nearly all his men into the city by one gate, taking with them, despite their protestations, Roy and Meroo and Old Faithful, while he himself, with but one or two troopers, Foster-father, Foster-mother, Head-nurse and the two children, entered by another and found lodging in the caravanserai as common travellers. Evidently, Foster-father surmised, it was thought best for some reason or another to conceal the fact that the Heir-to-Empire was being carried off to Kabul; and something happened that evening to make him certain that this was the case. It was dark ere they arrived, so the other travellers in the *serai* took little heed of the small party, especially as there were women

Flora Annie Steel

and children in it, and it is not polite in Eastern countries to take any notice of them. But while Head-nurse and Foster-mother were busy settling down the children's quilts in the little dark archway room, which was all the accommodation available, and Foster-father had gone to purchase them some milk for their supper, the little Prince and Princess, greatly excited at the novelty of their surroundings, wandered out into the dark square enclosure, where fires burned here and there in the open, lit by travellers who were cooking their evening meal. They stood by these watching what was going on with quick interest, answering questions that were put to them with frank smiles and laughter. Being dressed in heavy sheepskin outer coats to keep out the cold, no one guessed that they were other than they seemed, poor travellers' children, until at the end of a long row of picketed horses at the further end of the courtyard, Akbar saw Horse-chestnut, Foster-father's pony. Now Foster-father had only had time to tie the poor beast head and heel, so there the honest creature stood, looking very dejected, with emptiness before it, while the troopers' horses beside him were enjoying great bundles of green grass. The little fellow flushed up in a moment; he called loudly to a man who stood near:

"Ho! slave there! bring my pony grass—dost hear? and be quick!"

The man laughed. "Alah!" he said; "whose son be you to give orders that fashion?"

"Whose son?" echoed the child passionately. "I am—"

But Bija clung to his arm. "H'st, Mirak!" she whispered. "Remember what Head-nurse said that we were not to tell—"

Akbar stood irresolute; he was wise beyond his years. "But Horse-chestnut must not be hungry. I won't have it!—he shall have grass," he said angrily; then, without another word he walked up to the next horse, took a great armful of the grass that lay in front of it and scattered it before his favourite.

"So there! slave!" he cried defiantly with a stamp of his foot.

The man looked at him curiously, said nothing, but went over to some others and began to whisper.

A minute afterwards, Foster-father returning, found the children the centre of a little crowd eager in enquiry whence they came, whither they were going, and, ere he could get them safely to their quarters, the attention of the Captain of the Escort had been arrested, he came out frowning and fuming.

"We march again in an hour," he said angrily to Foster-father. "On thy head be it if thou can'st not keep thy young fighting cock in order—'twill be all over the town by midnight!"

Foster-father did not often let his temper get the better of his prudence, but he could not resist saying mildly: "Kingship is like the musk-bag, friend, that was broken at the royal child's birth. It diffuses its perfume over the habitable world, and none can mistake it."

The Captain of the Escort shrugged his shoulders. "Then it shall smell in the wilderness, friend; for I run no risks of rescue this side the passes. So bid the women give the young crowing cockerel his supper and prepare to start again. There will be a moon in another hour and we can push on. Meanwhile I go to warn the other folk where to rejoin us."

It was a bitter cold night. The wind blew keenly from the

Flora Annie Steel

snow before them, and by the time they reached a miserable village, high up on the slopes of the pass, every one save the two children was chilled to the bone; but they, well happed in all the coverings the fugitives could compass, were warm; Akbar, in Foster-father's arms, with Down, the cat, cuddled up beside him, and acting as a hot bottle! Once more there was plenty of fuel in the rude hut where they found shelter, and stiffened limbs and half-frosted fingers soon began to thaw. Tumbu, who had kept himself supple by, as usual, bounding about, was the only one of the party who did not doze off at once, now comparative comfort was reached.

But he was curiously restless. Over and over again he rose, went to the door and seemed to listen. Then he began to whine a little, then to scratch at the door as if he wanted to get out. Finally, finding no one paid any attention, he let loose one short, sharp bark, which awakened Head-nurse, who with an impatient look to see if her children had been disturbed, and an angry whisper, "Go, then! thou mean-born beast," rose softly, set open the door for a second, then closed it again, shivering with the chill blast that swept in. But Tumbu was out like a flash and disappeared in the darkness.

It must have been an hour afterward that every one's slumber was disturbed by the most insistent barking that ever was heard. Even Akbar, usually the soundest of sleepers, sat up and rubbed his eyes.

"The evil-dispositioned hound!" said Head-nurse in drowsy anger. "I deemed he had left us forever, and good riddance, too."

But little Prince Akbar, half awake, protested in defence of his dear dog.

"Tumbu only barks when he wants something, nurse; go and see what it is."

"A likely story!" cried Head-nurse.

"Well," interposed Foster-father philosophically, "some one must go if any one is to sleep."

Whereat he went to the door; but Tumbu on the doorstep refused to come in; he barked, bounced off, and returned the next minute to whine and bark again.

"He only wants something; go and see what it is," came Mirak's deep-toned voice. "I know he wants something."

"Lo! man alive!" grumbled Head-nurse; "shut the door whichever way it is. I perish with cold!"

Foster-father was a wise man, so to avoid further discussion he stepped out and shut the door behind him. Thus for a minute or two there was peace. Then Foster-father's voice rose urgently from outside.

"Open! I say open! Quick!"

Foster-mother flew to obey, and her husband staggered in, bearing some one in his arms. "God send the boy be not dead," he said as he laid down his burden.

It was Roy the Rajput!

"I found him quite close, frozen by the cold," he continued, as they set to work before the fire to rub the poor, stiff limbs and force a few drops of hot milk through the blue lips.

It was some time before a faint sigh, a quiver of the eyelids told that Roy was once more coming back to the world; but after that it was not long before he could sit up and tell them what had happened.

He had managed to evade the eyes of the troopers, and had arrived at the *serai* just after the startled party had left it; had followed on their traces until he had lost his way. In despair he had been stumbling along aimlessly when Tumbu had suddenly appeared. Following his lead, he had struggled on, gradually benumbed by cold, until at last his feet had failed him, and he remembered no more.

"Tumbu wanted Roy!" said little Prince Akbar gravely. "I told you he wanted something."

And Tumbu, hearing his name, roused his furry head from his furry paws and looked at his young master with his sharp, beady, black eyes, as who should say:

"Of course I did, because I knew you wanted him."

CHAPTER XII

SNOW AND ICE

The Captain of the Escort was not over pleased to find Roy when he came in the next morning, and said curtly that the boy, having found his way on foot, must make it on foot, and that none should wait for him. To this the Rajput lad made no demur. His long limbs on that hilly country were more than an equal even for Horse-chestnut's climbing powers, and the cold was so intense that it was a relief not to sit still on horseback. So he raced on ahead with Tumbu or held by Horse-chestnut's stirrup, and, as he ran, told stories to amuse the Heir-to-Empire; for neither of the nurses was in a fit state to do more than sit tight, tied by leathern belts to the troopers behind whom they rode.

About sunset time they arrived at a lonely shed at the beginning of the highest bit of the main road, which they were now obliged to take, as there was no other way over the mountains ahead of them. Here, at the end—as poor Head-nurse wailed—of the habitable world, the Captain of the Escort had expected to find the remainder of his men; but they were not there, and as his provisions were running short, he could not go on till they did arrive. So, in an ill humor, he ordered a halt, and the whole outwearied party hastily cooked themselves a meagre supper and lay down in hot haste for rest at last. And rest they had, for that night the snow, which had been threatening, began to fall, and by daylight a good nine inches lay on the ground. The children, who had never seen such thick snow before, were delighted; but Foster-father looked fearfully at the passes before them, while the Captain of the Escort fumed and fretted at the non-arrival of his men. Unless they came soon, he said, if more snow fell, the pass immediately in front of them might be closed for days. Not that there seemed much likelihood of further storm, for the sky was blue as blue, the air, though keen, pleasant. About noon, there being still no sign of the missing men with provisions, the captain became impatient, and told Foster-father curtly that he and his three troopers would ride back some fifteen miles to a village, where perchance the others were waiting, and that meanwhile the rest of them could wait till he returned; there were provisions enough for a day or two. Foster-father protested against being left alone in the snow with but a boy, two helpless women and two young children; but the Captain only laughed and rode off, taking with him Horse-chestnut, as a precaution, doubtless, against any attempt to escape with the Heir-to-Empire.

There was nothing to be done, Foster-father felt, save to wait with what patience he could; but his heart sank as, while Head-nurse and Foster-mother slept, outwearied by the past two days' fatigue, and the children under Roy's care played snowballs, he sat and watched the sky. At first there was only a cloud or two in the west; then a sudden wind sprang up and drove the fine, powdery snow in drifts. But still the sun shone, though it seemed to grow a little dimmer, a little paler; finally, about two hours after the others had left, Foster-father felt uncertain whether it was all drift that seemed to fill the air with a fine white film, or whether fresh snow was falling.

An hour later there was no doubt about it. Great flakes were circling down silently, the sun had vanished, all things had become grey. Head-nurse heaped up the fire, set a quilt before it for the children to play upon, and then opened out the wallets to see what she could find for supper. There was not much left, and she was about to knead up all the flour to bake hearth cakes when Foster-father crossed over to her and whispered:

"Half will do, sister; otherwise there may be none for to-morrow."

"None?" she echoed. "But they will be back—"

Foster-father pointed to the snow that, driven now by a rising wind, had drifted underneath the door. "Not through that, sister! We may have to stay here till the weather moderates, for none save friends will risk their lives, and these men love us not!"

But even as he spoke there was a bustling at the door, Tumbu flew forward, barking loudly, and in stumbled—

Old Faithful and Meroo the cook-boy!

They were heavily burdened, half-blinded by the snow, and they had a disquieting tale to tell. About twelve miles back, just as the snow began to fall, their party, which had been delayed on the main road by a flooded river, had come upon the Captain of the Escort and his three troopers. Then had ensued a hurried consultation, in which several of the men had flatly refused to go on in face of the coming storm. It was, they said, sheer madness. Better return to the nearest township and await better weather. As for the prisoners, they had food enough to keep life in them for a day or two, and after that they must take their chance. Whereupon Old

Faithful and Meroo had offered to go on, carrying some of the provisions they had with them, and trusting to be able to follow the tracks left by the horses in the snow. This had been agreed upon, and—here they were!

"For," as Old Faithful went on, "see you, I am not afraid of snow, having been with Babar the brave (on whom be peace) when he marched from Herat to Kabul and was nigh lost on the Great Zirrin pass."

Little Akbar, who was playing at cat's cradle with his sister, looked up eagerly. "Was Grand-dad ever in the snow? 'Cos if he was, he's quite sure to help us, for he ate all our sweeties, didn't he, Bija?"

The little girl shook her head and put her finger to her lip, in warning to him not to give away their secret; but Head-nurse was sharp.

"Ohe," said she, "so that was it! Listen, Foster-father! these babes set the platter for Firdoos Gita Makani—on whom be peace! Is not that good omen for us all?"

"Mayhap!" said Foster-father, clearing his throat cautiously, "and my heart is comforted also by the presence of Faithful, who was with the great king in his battle with snow and ice."

The Heir-to-Empire dropped his cat's cradle and went over to the old trooper and stood before him with grave, questioning eyes.

"Is it so, slave? Were you with Grand-dad in the snow?"

"Most-Honourable! I was," replied the old man boastfully, "and I remember as if 'twas yesterday—"

"Tell us the tale, trooper," interrupted Head-nurse. "'Twill hearten us all up ere we sleep, since there is naught else to be done."

"That will I, mother," replied Old Faithful with alacrity, "and in the very words of my revered master as written in that book of books, his Memoirs, which doubtless the most Learned-of-the-Universe will read some day."

Mirak, who was back at his cat's cradle, looked up with grave superiority.

"Nay, slave! They shall read it to Akbar. He will be King."

"Hark to him!" ejaculated Foster-mother, delighted. "His words are all fortunate."

"We have need of more fortune by works, not words, woman," said Foster-father sternly. "So proceed, friend Faithful; the recitation of brave deeds can never come amiss."

Old Faithful settled himself by the fire and began. "First you must know that Firdoos Gita Makani, or Babar the brave, had to get back to Kabul, because wicked men were waiting to be punished. Now, it was winter time, and none dreamed of travelling over the passes at that season. But Firdoos Gita Makani was not one to hold back when a thing had to be done. So we started, and this is what happened, in his own words:

"From the time we left Herat it snowed incessantly; the farther we advanced the deeper it became. After three days it reached above the stirrups. In places the horses' feet did not reach the ground; yet the snow continued to fall. One Bishai was our guide. I do not know whether it was from old age, or from his heart failing him, but having once lost the road, he never could find it again; so, as it was not to be found with all our exertions, we were brought to a complete stand. Seeing no other remedy, we returned back to a place where there was abundance of firewood, and despatched sixty or seventy chosen men to retrace our footsteps and find on lower ground any people who might be wintering there, and bring back another guide. We halted thus for three or four days awaiting the return of our messengers; but when they did appear it was without any one to show the way. Placing my reliance on God alone, therefore, I went on. For about a week we continued beating down the snow so as to form a road, only advancing two or three miles a day. Accompanied by ten or fifteen of my personal followers, I worked myself with the others. Every step we took forward we sank up to the middle, but still we went on, trampling till we got firm foothold. And as the first person wearied of the exertion, he stood back and another took his place. So, after a time, we managed to lead on a riderless horse. It generally sank to the stirrups, and after floundering on a dozen paces was worn out. But the second did better. Thus in this way the twenty or so of us managed to prepare a sort of road for the rest, who with hanging heads (though many of them had seemed our best men) advanced along it without even dismounting! But this was no time for reproof or authority. Every man of spirit hastens to such work of himself, and the rest do not count. In this way after three or four days we reached a cave at the foot of the Zirrin Pass. That day the wind and storm were dreadful; the snow fell in quantities; we all expected to meet death together. The snow was so deep, the path so narrow, the days were at shortest. The first of the troops reached the cave while it was yet daylight; but some men had to wait for morning on horseback. The cave seemed to be too small for all, so I would not go in. I felt that for me to be warm and comfortable while my men were in snow and drift; for me to sleep at my ease while my followers were in trouble and distress, would be unfair. I felt that whatever their sufferings might be, I ought to share them. So I took a hoe and dug down into the snow as deep as my breast; this gave me some shelter from the wind, and I sat down in the hole. By bedtime prayers the snow had fallen so fast that four inches of it had settled on my head—'"

Here Old Faithful paused and shook his head gravely. "His Majesty," he went on, "writes in the margin, 'That night I caught a cold in my ear.' It is only wonder he did not catch his death."

"But what happened next?" asked Akbar impatiently. "Did poor Grand-dad sit in the snow all night?"

"No, Most-Honourable. He goes on to say, 'The cave was properly explored and found to be large enough to hold us all. So I ordered all to go in, and thus we escaped from the terrible cold, snow, and drift, into a wonderfully warm, safe, comfortable place. And next morning the snow and tempest ceased and we moved on, trampling down the snow as before; but ere we quite got through the pass, night fell. Though the wind had fallen, the cold was dreadful, and several lost fingers, toes, even hands and feet from frostbite, as we waited for dawn in the open. As early as we could we moved down the glen, descending, without road, over difficult and precipitous places, the extreme depth of the snow enabling us to pass over countless dangers. Thus our enemy became our friend.

"'It was evening prayer time ere we got from the mouth of the valley, bedtime prayers when we reached the village of Auleng. The people carried us to their warm houses, brought out fat sheep for us, a superfluity of hay and grain for our horses, with abundance of wood to kindle our fires. To pass from the cold and snow into such a village with its warm houses, to find plenty of good food as we did after days of hunger is an enjoyment that can only be understood by those who have suffered similar hardship, have endured such heavy distress.'"

Old Faithful paused and sighed. "That is so like Firdoos Gita Makani," he said. "When danger was over he would sit down and write beautiful things about it; but when it was there he never seemed to think of anything but trampling it down."

"That is like all Kings," said Roy proudly, "and brave men are always Kings in danger."

But Foster-father was looking at the fire. "Abundance of fuel," he murmured, "that is what we have not."

"We shall not need it here, friend," replied the old trooper. "Meroo, remove that log; 'tis too hot as it is, and if the snow continues to drift as it was doing a while agone—" he moved to the door, which opened inward and set it wide. A great white wall reaching almost to the eaves showed filling up the doorway! "It is as I thought," he said; "we are prisoned here till the storm passes. Thank God we have provision enough for some days."

"And thanks to others also," put in Foster-father heartily; "but for thee and Meroo, old friend—"

"As Firdoos Gita Makani used to say," remarked the old man with an air of great virtue, "'Gratitude comes when danger has gone,' so she must wait a bit yet."

CHAPTER XIII

OVER THE PASS

Gratitude had longer to wait than even Foster-father, who always took a gloomy view of things, had thought for, since the next morning found the shed almost hidden beneath a snowdrift. Still, as Old Faithful remarked, it was not altogether to be regretted since the covering kept out the cold and allowed them to save their small store of firewood for cooking. The lack of light was, however, terrible until Old Faithful, whose experience with Babar the brave made him full of expedients, hit on the plan of setting Tumbu to work to dig out a hole through the drift, for they had nothing with them to use as a spade. What he did was to set the door wide, cut a narrow tunnel with his sword as far as he could reach in the banked-up snow, and thrust a bit of food in its farther end. Then Roy brought Tumbu and said:

"Fetch it out, good dog! fetch it out!" while Mirak and Bija looked on delightedly, calling, "Good dog! Dig it out! dig it out!" Tumbu, the most playful of animals, soon entered into the fun, and set to work shovelling out the snow till he found the food. Then another bit was thrust in, always in an upward direction.

"'Tis slow," said Old Faithful, "but not so slow as trampling

Flora Annie Steel

down a road!"

Not half so slow, for after a time Tumbu seemed to understand what they would be at, and needed no more bits of food to make him dig, but went on solidly, every now and again giving a yap just to make himself believe he really *was* digging something out. In fact, he got on so fast that Roy, who, as the slimmest of the party, had to keep the tunnel clear of the dug-out snow, had almost more to do than he could manage. It was frightfully exciting, and Mirak and Bija were dancing about, unable to keep still, when a sudden shaft of light that burst into the dark shed, and a furiously joyful barking that came down the funnel as if it had been a speaking trumpet, announced Tumbu's arrival in free air.

"Now, we shall do," said Old Faithful with much importance. "Lo! how one clever idea begets another. But for Firdoos Gita Makani trampling a road I should never have thought of a tunnel!"

Roy, however, was already hard at work improving on the idea by widening the way with Old Faithful's sword, being only let from doing more by Head-nurse's exclamation that the melting snow would flood the shed.

"Let be, boy!" said Foster-father; "the hot air from within, rising through the tunnel, will melt the sides by degrees. To-morrow will see it large enough for you, at any rate, to pass through."

And so it proved. Not next day, but the day after, not only Roy, but Mirak and Bija, had managed to climb up to the outer world by the notches which Roy cut in the snow walls.

It was a strange, chill world which they saw. Far as the eye could reach, nothing but snow, the air frosty and sharp, though the sun was shining once more. Mirak was keen to snowball, but Roy would not hear of it; the snow was melting with the faint heat of the mid-day sun, he said, and a step might make the frost film break, and down into the powdery drift they might go, never to come up again. So they only stood looking about them for a few minutes and then prepared to go back.

"Take care, my lord, take care!" cried Roy, as Mirak, who was preparing to descend legs foremost, as he had been told to do, suddenly looked up with a face full of mischief, let go with his hands, and pouf! disappeared down the slippery tunnel like a pea in a pea-shooter. A burst of laughter from below told them he had arrived safely, and nothing would suit Bija but to do likewise, Roy being still too tight a fit to slide quickly. In fact, the children were eager to climb up once more and do it again, but Head-nurse said she could not hear of it; their clothes were wet enough as it was; besides, it was most unlady-like for a real Princess!

The days, therefore, did not pass so uncomfortably, though pressing anxiety sat on Foster-father's honest face, and every time Roy returned from a climb up to outer air he would ask him if he had seen anything.

"Nothing," Roy would reply, "and the snow wastes but little, we are so high up."

At last one night, after the children were asleep, Foster-father summoned a council of war. It would not be wise, he said, to remain where they were, without making any effort at escape, until their provisions were exhausted. Then they would be helpless. Now they still had enough for two or three days, and it behooved them to make a push—but whither?

Flora Annie Steel

"Not back on our steps," advised Old Faithful. "Firdoos Gita Makani always said: 'No retreat till there is no advance.' Besides, see you, if we go down, the snow will be melting and give us no foothold. But at night the frost will hold on the pass. And it is but little farther to the next shelter; for, see you, I have come twice this way from Kandahar; but never the other way back. So my memory of land-marks—if there be any—would be nothing on the downward journey. But upward it might come to life. Again, upward there is less chance of missing the way, as all the valleys converge to the Pass, whereas downward they spread out in different directions."

In fact, there were so many points in favour of advance that the decision was made for it, and the next night settled on for the start. There were not many preparations to make except for the women, who had to bake what flour they had into hearth cakes. They had a little wheat and pulse, too, and this they roasted and tied up in the corners of their veils. Everything that was heavy had to be left behind, for they knew that even unburdened they might have difficulty in getting the frost film on the snow to bear their weight. It was a bright, starlight night when, the snow tunnel having been enlarged by Roy, regardless of flooding the shed, the whole party crept out and stood on the wide, snowy expanse. Tumbu was first, and with joyful yaps began to career about in circles curved like a comma, biting and snapping at the snow. Down came last, and *meaowed* piteously, lifting up first one cold foot, then another, and shaking it in disgust. Finally an idea seemed to come into her head; she made a bound toward Tumbu, and the next moment was on his back, clawing onto his fluffy black fur; whereat everybody laughed. So, with many a prayer for guidance, the little party set off, Old Faithful leading the way. At first they managed pretty well, though the men and women, being heavy, sank over the ankles at each step. But both Bija and Mirak, and even Roy, being light, found the surface hard enough to bear them; so they ran on ahead and chattered and laughed, the whole business being to them a huge joke. Thus an hour passed cheerfully enough; then Bija began to get tired, and Foster-father took her in his arms. The result sent his heart into his mouth with sudden fear, sudden certainty that no help could come that way. Even her slight additional weight sent him almost waist deep into the snow. He could scarcely move! And ere long the Heir-to-Empire would doubtless weary also; then what was to be done? For every hour after midnight would bring the thawing sun nearer and nearer; they might have to remain on the Pass till night brought frost again, and in that case what would become of the children?

Then suddenly his eye caught Tumbu, who was marching along sullenly, Down nestling, fast clawed in his broad, furry back. Could the dog carry a child? A creature with four feet had greater purchase of foothold than one with two.

"Roy," he said, "turn the cat off and put the Heir-to-Empire on the dog's back; he must be tired also."

Mirak, nothing loath, climbed quickly to his mount; but ere he had settled himself on its back Tumbu had begun to sink slowly. The little lad's weight was too much for even four feet; there was a struggle, over went the little Prince, and both he and Tumbu had to be picked up and set on their legs again on a fresh, unbroken place.

Foster-father looked in despair at Old Faithful, and for a minute no one said anything. Then the old man's face lit up. "Lo! I had forgotten it utterly, but the time and place bring memory back. Firdoos Gita Makani—who knew all things under the sun—had a favourite horse, that strained itself falling into a drift. They were for leaving it to die, but that did not suit Firdoos Gita Makani, who was kind to all God's creatures. So, having read of the like somewhere, he set us to make a sort of platform with our lances and blankets underneath the poor brute, and so we dragged him over the snow, until we reached a place where there was water and grass."

"We have no lances," said Foster-father, "and there is no wood." He looked around helplessly.

"My lord has a sword," put in Roy eagerly, "and so has Faithful. If he were to tie them crossways to the scabbards—"He had already thrown off his skin coat and was unwinding his long muslin waistband to tear it into strips to use as a cord.

"It is worth the trying, friend Foster-father," said Old Faithful, unbuckling his sword.

"Aye!" continued Roy, elated with the idea, "and Tumbu can drag it. He makes no mark on the snow, so it will be smooth and slippy—and the curved scabbards will be like runners."

His dexterous fingers were hard at work binding the long sword blades to place. Then a strip of woollen shawl was fastened to them as a seat, Meroo's turban served as harness, and in less time than could have been imagined the quaint sledge was ready for trial.

Mirak sat on it first. "Now then, Tumbu! Good dog!" said Roy in a flutter for fear of failure. Tumbu turned round, looked at his little master with a broad grin of red tongue and white teeth, gave a little grunt, and started.

The sledge slid on over the frozen snow quite easily!

"Now praise be to God!" cried Foster-father, overjoyed.

"And Grand-dad!" said the little Prince, who always listened to everything; "but I knew he would help us, didn't you, Bija?"

"But I want to go on the thing, too," she whimpered.

"Mayhap it might support them both," put in Head-nurse; "she is but a featherweight, and there is plenty of room."

Ere five minutes were over the little party, greatly heartened up by finding this unexpected way out of their difficulties, started once more, Roy encouraging Tumbu, who, in truth, seemed to feel his task quite a light one, while Foster-father, in his relief and gratitude, allowed Down, the cat, to creep once more inside his fur coat. Her weight made him sink a little farther into the snow, but he was strong, and felt he could have done more for the sake of the children's safety.

On and on they went, the frost film giving firmer foothold on the top of the pass, while the chill which always precedes dawn took away still more from the difficulty of Tumbu's task. In fact, the curved scabbards slipped over the hard snow as if it had been ice.

So they went on till a glimmer of dawn showed them that the summit had been reached, the downward slope begun. But still, far and near, nothing but snow was to be seen. Then suddenly, ahead of them, a shadow showed, a shambling shadow! Tumbu stopped dead, sniffed, then with a bound was off full tilt after it, the sledge, with the two children in it, flying behind him!

For an instant the others were too much astonished to speak. Then Roy, with frantic cries to Tumbu to come back, was off after them. In vain! As he crested a little rise he saw by the growing light a big brown Isabelline bear shambling along

Flora Annie Steel

contentedly, seeming to go no pace at all, yet gaining steadily on the sledge that was giving chase.

"I will follow as fast as I can!" panted the Rajput lad breath-lessly, as Foster-father, Meroo, and Old Faithful, hampered by their greater weight, ran up. "It is a bear; but they cannot catch it—and Tumbu will tire—then he always comes back. Follow you on my tracks with the women."

With that he was off like an arrow from a bow behind the bear, Tumbu, the sledge, the Heir-to-Empire and the Princess Bakshee Bani Begum, who by this time had all disappeared behind the hilly horizon.

CHAPTER XIV

IN THE VALLEY

Roy ran and ran and ran until he was breathless; yet still he ran, until little by little he recovered his breath again as wild animals do. Every moment he hoped to see Tumbu either returning or standing still, panting and waiting for the others to come up. But he saw nothing save, stretching away as far as the eye could reach, a smooth, not over steep, snowy slope. So far there was little fear of the sledge being overset.

Then, after he had run a long way, he paused, for there were now two tracks instead of one. The marks of the bear went up a little side valley, the marks of the sledge went down the slope. What could have happened? Had Tumbu in his haste missed the bear's trail? That was not likely. Having come so far, had he determined to go on? That was not likely either, unless the children had urged him forward. Knowing Mirak's bold, adventurous spirit, this seemed possible, and Roy's heart sank; but he started off running again, knowing that no matter what had happened he must follow his little master, and follow fast.

But as he ran downward and downward the frost film on the snow became less and less firm. The sun was rising now, and even its earliest rays seemed to melt his foothold, and he

Flora Annie Steel

began to sink at every step. The sledge, however, appeared from the faint marks it left to have slid on without difficulty. No doubt, he thought, because of the children's light weight, and because the platform between the swords and scabbards which supported them was so large; many times larger than his own feet! Why, even Tumbu's four broad, furry paws had sunk into the snow a little, and would doubtless have sunk more but for the pace at which he must have been going.

The sledge was the thing! How clever it was of Old Faithful to remember Firdoos Gita Makani's way of saving his horse; but after all, when one came to think of it, the thanks were due to Babar the brave for being a real King, kind-hearted to animals.

And now Roy's task became dangerous as well as hard, for every moment lessened the firmness of the ice film. And he was now running down a shallow valley, which was completely blocked up by drift, except in the very middle, where every now and again you got a glimpse of a roaring torrent—kept unfrozen by its snowy covering—hollowing its way downward; but for the most part it was invisible, the only sign of it being a roar, a tremble beneath your feet. Thus he was, as it were, on a snow bridge, of which the surface might at any moment give way. And that meant certain death in the dark pools below. In one place, indeed, he was all but lost; however, a wild leap landed him on safe ground, and with a gasp of fear, not for himself, but for the children ahead of him, he ran on, comforted by the sight of the sledge track going on and on.

After a while he had to cease running from sheer fatigue; but still he plodded on, telling himself that even half an hour would have made a difference in the snow. That where he found danger, the children might have found safety; and always before him that track of the scabbard-sledge showed him that so far, at any rate, all had gone well.

And then, as he turned a sharp curve in the shallow, snow-covered valley, he saw a little below him something that made him turn sick with fear. It was the sledge, empty, deserted! A second glance, however, showed him that it was not overset. Those who had been in it must have left it of their own accord; and the cause of this was soon made clear. Within a few yards the snow ended and a rocky descent began, down which the sledge could not have gone. So either Tumbu or the children had been wise; and they were still in front of him, but how far off who could tell? The sun was already high, hours must have passed since he first started in chase; but now that they were on foot there was some chance of overtaking them before anything dreadful happened.

In his hurry Roy almost flung himself from rock to rock down the descent; but he had to pause to take off his fur coat, for in this sheltered spot the sun beat shadelessly, the snow melted as he passed, the stones ran with moisture, and in the crannies of the rocks young green things were everywhere starting into growth. The past storm of bitter cold had ended winter; spring had begun. And now the rushing torrent, escaping finally from its snowy blanket, dashed over the boulders beside him, carrying with it great blocks of melting snow.

On and on he went, thinking the descent would never end, till at a turn he saw below him a tiny valley, just a sort of cup in the hills, through which the stream rushed, sparkling in the sunshine. The banks were still brown, but they were patched with great beds of rose-pink primula, blue gentian, and yellow dog pansies. And on a perfect carpet of these sat three dark figures! Never in his life was Roy so overjoyed. He forgot his fatigue, and ran on until he could plainly see Princess Bakshee Bani Begum making cowslip balls out of the pink primulas, the Heir-to-Empire contentedly munching a cold hearth cake, and giving bits of it to Tumbu, who, with his head cocked on one side, had evidently heard Roy's distant step. The next instant a furious barking showed that he was on the alert to defend his young charges, and Roy had to call to him again and again before he was satisfied that the newcomer was a friend.

"Why, what a long time you've been coming," said the Heir-to-Empire calmly. "We've had our breakfast, 'cos we couldn't wait any longer. You can't have come as fast as you could. No more would Tumbu, only we made him not be lazy, 'cos Head-nurse says—what is it she says, Bija?"

The little girl looked solemn. "She says every one should do everything as quick as ever they can. So we shouted at Tumbu and pulled his tail just a liddly-wee bit like the bullock drivers do. And then we had the loveliest ride, and Tumbu wasn't a bit cross; but he wouldn't go down the rocks and growled. So we had to get out and walk. And then we came here, and first of all we picked flowers; then I had hearth cakes and popcorn in my veil, and so we ate our breakfast, and then you came—and that's all, thank you!" She had just finished a lovely soft ball and she flung it full at the Heir-to-Empire. It hit him, but he took no notice. He was thinking of something else.

"But where," he began, and his little lip went down, "is Head-nurse—and Foster-father—and Foster-mother—and Old Faithful—and Meroo—and Down? What have you done with them, slave?"

He was half angry, half ready to cry, so Roy, though his own heart failed him as he thought of the dangers of the road, had to soothe and comfort him by saying, as cheerfully as he could, that they would come before long. But would they?

Now that the relief of finding the children were safe was over, poor Roy began to see the difficulties before him. If those others did not come, what would he, a mere lad, do? How could he care for his little master and mistress? They had had their breakfast, it is true—Roy forgot he had had none himself!—but what could they have for supper? He could not even think, he felt too giddy and tired even to sleep; so, after he had rolled his fur coat into a soft pillow for the little Prince and Princess, who were drowsy for their mid-day rest, and covered them over with their own, he sat with his head between his hands, his eyes closed, wishing he were not so stupid, wishing he could only think of something to do; for in reality he was quite wearied out. If the others did not come! Of course they might come at any moment; and yet the moments passed to minutes, the minutes to hours, while the children slept in the sunshine, and Roy felt that he was a fool.

And then something cold touched his hand. He opened his eyes and saw that it was Tumbu's nose; Tumbu, who had something strange in his mouth—something like a rabbit and yet like a squirrel!

In reality it was a fresh-killed young marmot, an animal that lives amid the snow and ice and rocks of the very highest hills. Tumbu, having handed over charge of the children, must have gone off on his own hunting, found a colony of the quaint creatures, and, as usual, brought home his bag! Roy did not in the least know what the marmot was, but he saw it was something to eat! The relief was too much for him! Here, at least, was supper. He flung his arms round Tumbu's neck and burst into tears, murmuring with choking sobs that he, Roy, had been foolish, but Tumbu was a wise, wise, good doggie. And so he was!

After this Roy felt better, and having, as all Indian boys used

Flora Annie Steel

to have in those days, a flint and steel with him, began to look around for fuel with which to light a fire and cook the supper. There were, of course, no trees and no bushes; but right away at the farther end of the long valley there were some patches of very dark green. They did not look promising, but he would go and see. They proved to be a creeping sort of evergreen plant that trailed its stiff branches right on the very ground. He picked a bit, and on trying to light it, found to his surprise, that it blazed up in a fierce flame. For it was juniper, and so full of resin.

He now had the possibility of fire, so that evening the little cup in the hills held quite comfortable encampment.

Roy had brought down the sledge, and using the swords and their scabbards as supports, had made a lean-to tent against a warm rock out of the strip of shawl. In this he had strewn juniper branches to make a soft bed, and the children could just creep into it. Then they had the marmot, roasted in its skin, for supper, and all the three were too hungry to ask themselves if marmot flesh was as toothsome as rabbit or as bitter as squirrel! And Tumbu ate the bones with an air as if he would say, "It is not bad, but to-morrow I must catch two marmots."

After that there was peace and quiet in the camp, Roy sitting beside the fire and making it blaze up every now and again by putting on a fresh juniper branch. For he knew that since the others had not arrived by daylight, they must either all have perished on the road or else be waiting until the cold of night once more froze the ice-film on the snow. In this case the firelight seen from afar might be a guide.

So the night passed. More than once Roy fell asleep, for despite his care the smoke of the juniper branches could not quite be avoided, and that, every one knows, is terribly sleepifying. He woke every time, however, before the fire was quite out, and hastened to send up a flare of flame. As he did so the last time it was answered by a *hulloo* from the rocks above, and shortly afterward Meroo, the scullion's, blubbering voice could be heard as he uttered thanks to Heaven.

"And the others?" asked Roy anxiously, as out of the darkness Meroo appeared and cast himself at the lad's feet, bellowing joy.

"They come, they come! They are but a short way back. I saw the fire, and the sight of it warmed the cockles of my heart! Lo! I shall cook once more! I shall not die hungry in the wilderness. Nay! go not," for Roy was starting up. "True! the women are nigh dead, and Foster-father hath his fingers frost-bitten, but—nay, put more flame to the fire, boy! It is the fire they need!"

He was half beside himself, but he was right. As the fresh juniper branches blazed up Head-nurse came tottering and stumbling into its light. Roy sprang to help her, but she pushed him aside.

"The Heir-to-Empire?" she muttered, her lips almost refusing to form the words. "The Heir-to-Empire, the Admired-of-the-World—"

Roy pointed to the little tent. "There! Safe! Well! Asleep!" he cried; and the poor woman with a sob sank as she stood, and lay prone muttering long strings of titles.

Before a minute had passed Foster-father and Foster-mother struggled into the circle of light, and after a word of question and reply, sank down also.

Flora Annie Steel

Then there was a long pause, but no sign came of good Old Faithful's tall, gaunt figure. At last Roy spoke.

"Faithful?" he asked in a low whisper. "What of him?"

There was no answer at first; only Foster-father covered his face with his hands. At last he spoke gently.

"He was faithful to death. He was going first, as ever, cheering us all with his sayings of Firdoos Gita Makani. I saw him there one moment turning to tell us words of wisdom—the next the snow bridge had given way beneath his feet and he was gone. We waited on the bank of the awful chasm for a long time, but there was no sound save the roaring of the stream below. Firdoos Gita Makani, his master, had called him. Peace be with them both!"

CHAPTER XV

DEAREST-LADY

For two whole days the little party was too weary even to attempt a move. They had some provisions with them, and Tumbu, as good as his word, brought in more and more marmots; for being unaccustomed to dogs, they were easily caught.

The death of Old Faithful weighed upon the spirits of all, and for the first twelve hours or so the Heir-to-Empire was inconsolable for the loss of his beloved cat; for Foster-father had found it impossible to carry Down farther, and she had remained behind in the snow, protesting piteously. It was a terrible grief, and the child had almost wept himself sick, when, to every one's surprise and delight, Mistress Down was seen walking sedately across the flowers, her bushy tail carried very high, not one hair of her silky white coat awry. She took no notice of anybody, but passed to the fire, sat down beside it with stiff dignity, curled her tail round her paws, yawned and then began to purr gently. It was as if nothing had happened. And she certainly was not hungry, for she turned up her dainty nose at Tumbu's marmot bones.

"Cats," said Head-nurse, who had just awakened from a long sleep of many hours, "are not to be counted as other beasts.

Having nine lives, they could afford to lose one; but they never do. They always fall on their feet. It is the way of the world; the more you have the more you get. Still, I am glad she has returned; and I wish there were a chance of others turning up also," she added with a sigh.

The Heir-to-Empire looked up gravely. "But Faithful can't come back, you know. He went to help Grand-dad to help us."

"Hark to the innocent," cried Foster-mother, half in smiles, half in tears, "but it is true. If ever poor mortals were watched over by saints in Paradise, we were; and for my part if ever I get to Kabul, my duty shall be paid to the tomb of Firdoos Gita Makani—on whom be peace."

"Amen!" added her husband devoutly; "but for the memory of that good man we should not be here now."

It was on the third day that leaving Meroo in charge for a few hours Foster-father and Roy set off to explore. They were fortunate in finding some shepherds' huts within a walking distance for even footsore women, and returned ere nightfall with a skin bag of fresh milk.

Early next morning, therefore, they all set off, Roy girding on dead Faithful's sword from the sledge that was wanted no more, and from that moment feeling himself indeed bodyguard to the Heir-to-Empire.

Once they had reached safety from starvation in the shepherds' huts, a great desire for rest came upon them all; and for three whole days they did nothing but eat, and sleep, and rejoice in the early spring sunshine, and the early spring flowers. For the late snap of extreme cold had passed and every green thing was hurrying to be ahead of its neighbour.

Bija made endless cowslip balls out of the beautiful rose-pink primulas, while Roy and Mirak, following the shepherds' boys, came back with their hands full of young rhubarb shoots and green fern croziers, which they ate like asparagus. But this sort of thing could not last long, since they were close to the caravan route from Kandahar to Kabul; and sure enough, no sooner had the snow on the uplands melted than travellers began to pass through.

Thus news that the little party had escaped death soon filtered from mouth to mouth, till it reached the Captain of the Escort, and ere long Foster-father found himself and those in his care once more semi-prisoners on their way to cruel brother Kumran; all the more cruel, doubtless, because King Humayon had already begun the siege of Kandahar, believing his little son to be still within its walls.

Now Kumran was a far cleverer fellow than his brother Askurry; but there was in him a love of deceit for deceit's sake, which spoiled all his cleverness, for it made him uncertain what he would do in the end. This indeed is always the case with deceitful people. They know that what they say and do is *not* straightforward and true, and so they are like sailors without a compass. They have no fixed pole by which to steer.

And, in addition, Kumran liked to be considered clever; so he was always outwardly very courteous, very polite, very charming; but what he was within none could say for long.

Thus Foster-father's heart sank within him, when in the distance, down the rocky ravine through which the Kabul River dashes, and along which the caravan road took its high-perched way, he saw the battlemented wall of the city, cresting the low hills on which the town was built. It was a fully fortified town through which the river ran, and at its extreme end, commanding the wider plain below, stood the citadel called the Bala Hissar or High Fort. To reach this the travellers had to cross the iron bridge and wend their way through the narrow bazaars.

Such wonderful bazaars as they were, too! Crowded with tiny dark arched shops, like caverns, full to the brim with Persian silk carpets, furs from the north, turquoises and all kinds of precious stones from out-of-the-way places with unpronounceable names. And there were such a quantity of cats! Grey Persian cats and white ones, and tabbies and black cats who sat on the balconies and stared at Down as she lay on Horse-chestnut's broad, wavy back. For the Captain of the Escort had found out what an excellent creature the old pony was, and had brought it along with him.

The High Fort was a huge place with great gardens within its battlements and several separate palaces. Here, to Foster-father's unbounded delight, they found that Prince Kumran was himself away, having gone out with a small body of men to the Kandahar frontier, where King Humayon's arrival had aroused loyalty. But what was still more cheering was the news that he had left orders for the Heir-to-Empire and his sister to be handed over on arrival to the charge of Dearest-Lady! Foster-father could hardly believe his ears; for Dearest-Lady (as she was always called by all her family, by all her nephews and nieces, by all her grand nephews and nieces, and cousins, and every one who was lucky enough to belong to her) was simply—Well! what was she not? Wise, and gentle, and good, and clever—all this and more. She was the sort of Dearest-Lady who lived so long in the hearts of those who knew her, that, years after she was dead they would say, if there was any difficult point to be settled—"We wonder what Dearest-Lady would have said?"

She was old, of course, for she was Babar the Brave's elder

sister; the sister to whom he had been devoted, who had always been to him also "his Dearest-One." Now, when you come to think of it, boys and girls, that is a nice sort of fame to have—to remain for—let me see how many hundred years?—nearly four—Dearest-Lady, or Dearest-Gentleman to all the world.

This Dearest-Lady was, of course, the Heir-to-Empire's grand-aunt, and the mere sound of her name was enough to calm Foster-father's fears. Even Head-nurse, though she sniffed a little and said she had heard tell that the Khanzada Khanum was a trifle careless of ceremonials, was satisfied. There was no doubt that she was the Highest-Born-in-the-Land.

As for little Prince Akbar himself, he only opened his big, grave eyes widely when the tall white figure clasped him closely in its arms and kissed his hair softly.

"So like his grandfather," she murmured, "so like! so like!— the very hands, the very feet—so strong, so shapely." And both in turn felt the touch of the soft old lips. "And thou, too, small maiden," she continued kindly, "welcome to one who has never yet let it be said in her hearing that God made women weaker than man! Thou shalt learn here to be proud thou wast born a girl. And you also, Nurse! Bring cooling sherbets, slaves, while she tells me all that has happened."

Then she sat and listened while Head-nurse told the tale of what had happened, and her faded, gay, old face flashed and sparkled and grew grave by turns.

"But where is Tumbu?" she interrupted, "and where is Down? Bring them hither, slaves! Lo! I love all animals, as my dear brother did!"

Flora Annie Steel

And she laughed over their doings, and wept over Old Faithful's death, while Bija and Mirak sat cuddled up close beside her, listening also and enjoying the tale of their own adventures as if they had happened to other children!

"Surely," she said softly when Head-nurse ended, "my dearest brother—on whom be peace—must have protected them! Lo! Mirak! and Bija—for I shall call you naught else since they are sweet kindly names, better than fine sounding titles—this very afternoon ye shall come with me to the garden he loved, and where his earthly form lies at rest, and lay flowers on his grave for thanks. Since he loved flowers as he loved everything."

So that evening, about an hour before sunset time, they were all carried in litters to the Garden of the New Year, about a mile beyond the city. It was a most peaceful, lovely spot, right up on the hillside with a splendid view from it of valley and mountain and river. A fresh bubbling spring ran through it, and beneath the Judas trees, whose leafless branches were flushed with pink blossoms, stretched great carpets of spring flowers.

"Pluck him yonder tulips, Mirak," said Dearest-Lady with a smile. "He loved to count their kinds and those—as he wrote —are 'yellow, double, and scented like a rose'!"

And the boy who was to grow to be a greater man even than his grandfather, though he could scarcely be a more lovable one, plucked a posy of the tulips and laid them on the plain marble slab which bore nothing but the words, "Heaven is the eternal home of the Emperor Babar." And when Bija, with many a little feminine ceremonial, had deposited her nosegay of sweet violets, and Head-nurse and Foster-mother had offered up their respects, they all went and sat down on a grassy spot, and Dearest-Lady, who was always full of youthful curiosities concerning all things, began to question Roy, who as a mere lad had been allowed to come with them, as to what he could remember of the time before he was picked up in the desert.

"Hold my hand, child, and think," she said at last, "mayhap it may come to thee then. The touch of kinship has power, and if I do not mistake me, there is that in thy blood that is in mine—royalty!"

So she clasped Roy's slim long-fingered hand and held it tight, and the boy's face changed, his eyes grew startled, he shivered slightly.

"Yea!" he said, "now I do remember. Mother was like you, and she told me I had the mark of Kingship strong enough, for all the rebels might say—" As he spoke, he drew down his loose garments, and there upon the clear olive of his breast, just above the heart, showed a small dark stain.

Dearest-Lady bent close to look at it. "What is't?" she asked.

"Mother said it was the sign of uttermost truth, and that we all had it," he replied, speaking dreamily.

"But who were we?" persisted Dearest-Lady, her kind eyes on the lad's.

Just at that moment, however, Tumbu, who had, of course, accompanied them, burst out with a series of shrill, short barks, and Roy was on his feet in a second, his hand on Old Faithful's sword, lest any newcomer might bring danger to his little master. But as it turned out Tumbu was only excited by a water-rat! All the same the interruption prevented Dearest-Lady's question from being answered, for the spell was broken.

Flora Annie Steel

"Yea! thou wilt be true to the very uttermost, of that I am sure," said Dearest-Lady, half pleased, half amused at the young Rajput's quick leap to arms, "and so long as I have charge of the Heir-to-Empire thou shalt be his esquire. So go call the litter-men, boy, it is time we returned. I must remember I am gaoler as well as grand-aunt."

CHAPTER XVI

CRUEL BROTHER KUMRAN

If Dearest-Lady was in truth a gaoler, she was a very kind one, and her prison the pleasantest prison in the world. It would take too long to tell how happily the next four months passed, not only for the two children, but for Roy and Foster-father, Head-nurse and Foster-mother. Even misshapen Meroo, in the kitchen, felt the better for helping to cook the Khanzada Khanum's dinner. For that was one of Dearest-Lady's virtues, she always made people feel contented, and as if they were doing the right thing. So even Prince Kumran, when he returned to Kabul, though he frowned at the big, bold, frank-faced boy who claimed to be the Heir-to-an-Empire which his own fingers itched to have, did not feel inclined to interfere with his aunt. The truth being that, like the rest of the family, he loved and trusted her beyond measure; perhaps more than did any of his brothers, since she had brought him up as a child. And she, in her turn, though she knew his faults, though she not only bewailed them, but resented them, at times most fiercely, could not forget that he had been her nursling, could not forget, above all, that he was her dear brother Babar's son.

Thus all went smoothly in the Bala Hissar, where young Prince Akbar, now close on three years old, looked and

Flora Annie Steel

talked and acted like one of six. This same strength of his was always getting him into scrapes with people who did not believe he was so young, or, knowing him to be so young, did not believe him to be so strong!

He played a similar trick to the one he had played on cousin Yakoob at Kandahar on his big cousin Ibrahim, Prince Kumran's son. It was about a fine kettledrum all tasselled in royal fashion, with gold and silver, that Ibrahim's father had given him. Being a selfish boy, he would not allow Akbar to touch it; whereupon the Heir-to-Empire, after a brief tussle, carried off the kettledrum and beat it loudly through the palace!

Kumran hearing of this was very angry, for the beating of a kettledrum is a sign of Empire.

"Keep that young fighting cock of thine in better order, madam," he said to his aunt, "or I shall have to find him a sterner gaoler."

Whereupon she flashed out and told him fairly that short of killing the child, and for that crime even *he* was not pre- pared, there was no way of preventing the Heir-to-Empire from being what he was, a born king. That was her way of quelling Kumran. By boldly setting aside the thought of murder as impossible, she hoped to make it so; but she was not sure, and after this she kept Mirak and Bija under control.

It was not much good, however, when just as autumn was coming on news arrived from Kandahar that Humayon had at last succeeded in taking the city, and, disappointed in not finding his son in the palace, was preparing to march on Kabul.

Then the worst side of Prince Kumran showed itself at once. Like all deceitful people, he was a coward at heart, and cowardice made him think of immediate revenge upon his victorious brother. Of what use would even two victories be to him if the Heir-to-Empire was beyond recall?

So Kumran's charming polished manner vanished in an instant, and one day, without any warning, little Mirak, playing in the garden, was kidnapped by two stalwart Abyssinian slaves and carried off, howling horribly and fighting with his fists, to the palace where Kumran's wife lived. Tumbu, who was with him at the time, made a gallant show of resistance, and actually bit one of the kidnapper's calves to the bone; but when he found himself confronted with a whole regiment of armed men who ran out to their assistance, he gave up the hopeless fight, and flew off to tell Roy what had happened. And Roy, missing his little master, fled to tell Dearest-Lady. Her face paled, but she did not hesitate.

"My litter! page!" she cried, and drawing her white veil closer round her, she went straight to the audience hall, where Kumran was receiving his nobles; her great age, her great nobility, giving her a right, even as a woman, to appear amongst them.

All eyes turned to her tall, upright, slim figure, every ear thrilled to the tones of her clear voice.

"By what right," she asked, "has Kumran, the nephew I have nurtured, stolen from my care the son of his elder brother, the Heir to that Empire which Babar the Brave gave, dying, into the hands of Humayon, his eldest son? I say there can be no right; and if it be wrong then will God's curse light on the man who undoes his father's work. Lo! he is worse than parricide, for he would kill that for which his father gave his life."

Flora Annie Steel

Now this appeal was a very strong one; for the story of how Babar the Brave gave up his own life to save that of his darling son, Humayon, is one of the most touching tales in Indian history, and none of Babar's immediate family could even think of it without strong emotion. So it was Kumran's turn to grow pale.

"August lady," he replied, evading her question, "this is a matter of policy with which women have naught to do. King Humayon hath taken Kandahar, he hath imprisoned and degraded his brother Askurry, and for this, I, Kumran, challenge him!"

"And wherefore?" asked Dearest-Lady boldly. "Did not Askurry deserve it? Nay! did he not deserve death? Did he not steal the King-of-Empire? Did he not defy the king? Did he not send the Heir-to-Empire away, instead of returning him to his father's keeping? I tell you, nephew Kumran, that your father, Babar the Brave, Babar the Kindly, Babar the Generous, Babar the Just, whom all men loved for his mercy, would have given *death* for such faults—and given it rightly. And will you, like a fool, court death also?" She looked round the assembly to see many a sullen, suspicious face, and understood that danger lay close at hand. So her resolution was taken in a moment. "See you!" she went on, "nothing has been done yet to make forgiveness impossible. Well! I—Khanzada Khanum,—old as I am, will go forth to meet King Humayon and plead thy cause. I will ask what boon you wish, and I promise it shall be yours. Humayon will give much in exchange for his son, and none have ever denied me anything. Shall it be so?" Then seeing hesitation she put in a crafty word: "There will be time afterwards for—anything—"

Kumran looked round his nobles, then into his own heart. What he saw there was such a tissue of lies and deceit that he could find no clear decision; so, as usual, he temporised. "It is worth a trial," he murmured. "I might ask for much."

"Ask for all and everything," said Dearest-Lady, who felt she had gained her point; "I make but one condition. The child must remain unharmed until I return."

Again Kumran hesitated. Again he looked in his own heart. Again he found no clear cause for decision there; so he said doubtfully:

"Until you return?"

"Nay! swear it," came the high, insistent voice. "Say before them all, 'By the memory of my dear father no harm shall come to the child ere you return.'"

Half unwillingly Kumran repeated the words and Dearest-Lady gave a sigh of relief. She had gained her point. But now that she had to face the consequences of her offer to go forth and meet Humayon her heart sank within her; for she was very old and not over strong. The journey was long; winter was coming on fast. Still it had to be done, and at once. For Kumran's promise of safety to the Heir-to-Empire was only *during her absence*, and who knew whether his craft might not claim freedom to do as he chose ere she started!

So she made her arrangements for that very evening, and she had much to do. To begin with she must see the Heir-to-Empire the very last thing, and make certain that he was well cared for. Then she had to arrange for the safety and comfort of Head-nurse, Foster-mother and little Bija, for it was unlikely they would be allowed to be with the little Prince. He must, however, have some one with him to whom the child was accustomed, and Roy, being still quite a lad, might not be considered dangerous. Then his gift of story-telling might make the ladies in the women's apartments more inclined to have him. Anyhow she must try her best to secure his stopping with his young master, and to this end she ordered him some fine clothes and gave him a finely bedizened lute; for since he came to Kabul they had found out that he could play the *vina* beautifully.

Thus just before sunsetting, leaving poor Head-nurse and Foster-mother in floods of tears, while poor little Bija was sobbing her very heart out, and good dog Tumbu was slowly wagging his tail as his eyes asked sorrowfully if he might not come, too, she started on her journey, going round by the Chief Palace on her way.

Now, Dearest-Lady's visits were considered to be an honour, so she had no difficulty in gaining admittance. And once inside the women's apartments she simply turned to the first attendant and said curtly that she had come to see the Heir-to-Empire and say farewell to him; therefore he must either be brought to her or she must go to him. Boldness succeeded, as it always does, and she was shown into a room where she found little Prince Akbar playing contentedly with Down the cat, who was running about after a ball like a young kitten. She stopped when she saw Dearest-Lady, and giving an apologetic *miaow*, as who should say, "I was obliged to amuse him somehow," settled herself down on the rug and began as usual to purr. Of course Mirak forgot all about her in his joy at seeing Dearest-Lady and Roy, and it was some time before the former could ask the attendant how the cat had managed to get there.

"Highness," said the woman, "it is impossible to keep cats out if they want to come in. She appeared at the window three times, and three times I put her downstairs. Then I gave in. It is no use quarrelling with cats."

Meanwhile notice of Her Highness Dearest-Lady's arrival had reached Kumran's wife and she hastened to little Akbar's prison room. But once more Dearest-Lady was bold and took the first word.

"I came to bid the boy farewell, content to trust him to thy kind care, my niece," she said; "and also to leave with him this Rajput singer, who has the art of amusing the child—and other folk also. Roy! sing us one of thy tales, that the Princess may hear thee."

And Roy, knowing his part, sang as he had never sung before. "I will sing of how the palm squirrels helped the Great Ram to find his wife, Sita the Peerless, whom the wicked Giant Ravana had carried off. We sing it to the squirrels when we feed them in our country. Perhaps Her Highness does not know what a palm squirrel is. It is tiny, tiny, no bigger than a rat, but it has a bushy tail and four dark stripes like finger marks down its goldy-coloured back. And it never does anything but play, is never anything but happy; and this is why":

Then he smote the strings of the *vina* till they thrilled again, and began, his high voice warbling and carolling like a summer bird.

"Pretty! Pretty! Pretty! are you there, my sweet,
In your leafy seat, where the branches meet?
Wasting all the sunny hours
Pulling down the mango flowers
With your dainty feet.

"Pretty, prettiest thing yawning as you lie
Watching with glad eye, busy life go by.
Not the tiniest sense of duty
In your careless days, my beauty,

Flora Annie Steel

'Neath the cloudless sky.

"Happiest, merriest ways,
Knowing no gainsays, so the story says,
Since the Great Ram loved and blessed you,
With his care-worn hand caressed you,
In the olden days.

"Then, when he was seeking Sita, peerless maid,
By his foes dismayed, Ram, her lover, bade
All the beasts and birds and fishes
Leave their play to do his wishes,
Fight to give him aid.

"And the golden squirrel sprang at his behest,
Nestled to his breast, first to join the quest.
But Great Ram's grave eyes grew tender,
Smiled upon the warrior slender,
Braver than the rest!

"'Nay! thou art too pretty! fearless little heart,
Thou should'st have no part in Strife's bitter art;
Live to show man, worn and weary,
One blythe soul for ever cheery,
Free from sorrow's smart.'"

"Laid his kind hand softly on its golden hair,
So palm squirrels bear, where Ram's fingers were,
Four dark shadows on them, showing
Gladdest life must lose its glowing
From the touch of care.

"So the squirrels' birthright is to want for naught,
Have no grief or thought, know not 'must' or 'ought.'
Yet upon their gold there lingers
Shades of care, that Great Ram's fingers

For their blessing wrought."

"*Wah! Wah!*" cried the Queen, delighted. "He can stop if he likes."

Ten minutes after Roy had finished his song Dearest-Lady's litter paused for a moment on a high-perched corner of the road towards Kandahar, to give her a last look of the fair city of Kabul. Her bright old face was bright still, undimmed by care. She was old and frail, she was going a wearisome, trying journey; yet, for the present, she knew that she had saved the Heir-to-Empire's life. That at any rate was secure until she returned—and she might never return! The thought made her smile. "Forward, slaves!" she cried cheerfully, and Kabul, the city she loved so well, was left behind without one regret.

And she was right. She had saved the Heir-to-Empire's life; for at that very minute the door of little Prince Akbar's room opened wide, and Roy starting up found himself face to face with cruel Uncle Kumran followed by two men with drawn swords. And, alas for Roy! he had no sword to draw, for Old Faithful's sabre did not fit the disguise of a Rajput bard. Despite that, he stepped forward boldly, though his heart beat to suffocation. For Kumran's face was cruel indeed.

Still, for one second, the latter's attention was distracted. He had wanted no witnesses to what he meant to do.

"How camest thou hither, slave?" he asked fiercely.

And Roy gave him back the simple truth, no more, no less; but it was sufficient.

"Her Highness Khanzada Khanum brought me hither to be with the Heir-to-Empire ere she left at sunset."

Kumran started back. "Left? Hath she left already?" he asked, his face paling. So he stood for a moment irresolute, the words of his own oath pealing through his brain, "By the memory of my father I promise." That was not one which any son of Babar's was ever likely to break. "Sheath your swords, fools!" he said at last bitterly; "they are not needed. I am not the first man who has been outwitted by a woman."

CHAPTER XVII

IMPRISONMENT

But if Kumran was let and hindered by his oath from actually killing the Heir-to-Empire in cold blood, or, in lesser degree, from treating him so harshly that he might die, he did not feel so bound towards the others; and being cruel by nature, he set to work upon them at once. Foster-father he sent to the State prison, which was down a well in the big courtyard. There were two of these prison-wells, in which the water was reached by a flight of steep steps, and where dark, underground cells opened on to the deep silent pool. They were terribly damp, but here poor Foster-father had to drag out long, miserable days, cut off even from news of the others. Until one day, just when the sentry was eating his mid-day meal, he heard a violent barking, and by swinging himself up by the bars of the tiny shaft of the well he could just get a glimpse of Tumbu on the steps. Why had he come? Perhaps he had been sent; if so he would come again at the same time. All that night Foster-father lay awake, feverishly wondering what Tumbu had meant, and all the next morning, having no means of telling the time, he waited and waited anxiously, until, just as he was beginning to give up hope, the familiar bark echoed down the well, and there was good old Tumbu on the steps! So he must have been sent by some one; and therefore some one must be alive and desire him to

Flora Annie Steel

know the fact.

In truth, both his wife, Foster-mother, and Head-nurse had been racking their brains how to find out where either the Heir-to-Empire or Foster-father were imprisoned until little Bija had said, "Tell Tumbu to seek for them. If you show him Mirak's cap and say, 'Go seek,' he will go."

And so he did; but it was a long, long time before he found out where Mirak had hidden himself, for he had gone to the big palace in a litter, and so had left no trace. Then little Bija came to the rescue once more.

"You say, Foster-mother, that you feel sure that Down must have gone away to keep Mirak company. Now she *can't* be prisoned, 'cos cats won't be caught unless they want to be caught, and she doesn't want to be, *of course*. So she must be going about, so why don't you tell Tumbu to seek for Down; then we should find where Mirak was."

"But we haven't got anything of Down's to show him," argued Foster-mother. And that was a puzzler.

At last Head-nurse said, "I believe all cats have the same smell, else why do all dogs go after all cats? At any rate, it would be worth trying."

So they got a fine, large, handsome white cat in the bazaar, and said to Tumbu, "Go seek!" And then there was the most awful scrimmage that ever was seen. Tumbu was after the cat in a second, and the cat jumped for protection on Head-nurse, and Head-nurse howled, while Tumbu deafened everybody by yowls; for the cat had caught him on the nose! Peace was not restored till pussy had made her escape back to the bazaar through the window.

"That was not a success," sighed poor Head-nurse as she put herself tidy; but after all it was not such a failure, since, either from putting two and two together, or by mere chance, Tumbu appeared the very next day barking and frolicking after his usual fashion when he wanted them to go out, and then led them straight to a lonely corner of the palace garden, whence, looking upwards, they could plainly see Down seated on a narrow window sill. And the next moment, hearing the familiar bark, who should pop his head out of the window but Roy!

"All's well," he whispered rapidly seeing them below him; then withdrew his head swiftly. For he had determined never by anything or in any way to risk being sent away from the little Heir-to-Empire.

But the others were more than satisfied with the whisper.

"Now," said little Bija, who was beginning to manage her nurses, "Tumbu must find Foster-father and tell *him*." And this, we have seen, he did.

Even so, with the daily content of knowing that all were at least safe, the time passed with deadly slowness, for the days grew to weeks, the weeks to months, bringing no change. Denied, as he was, the outdoor life, the fresh air to which he had been accustomed, little Prince Akbar grew pale and thin. But his spirits did not flag, and he would laugh over the tale of how Rajah Rasalu swung the Seventy Maidens as heartily as ever, though sometimes his little lip would go down and he would say, "If Bija were only here I'd never ask her to tumble down. I would go on swinging till she wanted me to stop."

So the winter came on, but still Dearest-Lady did not return. A letter had come from her saying she had reached Kandahar

Flora Annie Steel

in safety—that she was staying in the Kar Garden outside the town which her father had planted—that King Humayon was not angry—that he had already forgiven Prince Askurry—that Kumran had nothing to fear if he only kept to his promise.

The prisoners, of course, knew nothing of this letter, but the effect of it showed in a greater freedom. Foster-father was moved to a more comfortable dungeon and Bija, Head-nurse and Foster-mother were allowed to go and see the Heir-to-Empire. Their delight may be imagined, and even Tumbu shared in the joy, for, when he was refused admittance and left down below, he dashed up the stairs, evading the sentries and barked furiously at the door to be let in. And the meeting between him and Mirak was so pretty that the sentry had not the heart to insist on poor doggie going down again. And this, in its way, was a good thing, for it was the beginning of a sort of friendship between the young Prince and this parti-cular Afghan sentry. Sometimes, after he had been relieved, he would come up to the little captive's room for a bit, and listen to Roy's stories, or tell a few in his turn; for he had wandered about, over half India, giving the use of his sword to any one who would pay him well for it.

"Lo! I have not heard that tale since I was in Rajputana!" he said one day after Roy had been singing an old-world legend of fighting days. "It was an old Brahman of Suryamer told it me of the Sun-Heroes."

Roy's face flushed up in a second. "Suryamer is mine!" he said proudly; "I am of the Sun-Heroes!"

Then he started to his feet, pale as ashes. "I have remembered! I have remembered at last," he said almost with a cry. "It is true! I was Rajah of Suryamer! It has come back to me at last!"

Then as suddenly he crouched down again and covered his face with both hands.

"Roy!" said little Prince Akbar gravely. "Why should you cry because you are a King? I don't."

The sentry laughed. "By my word," he remarked, "there is a blessed pair of you Kings!"

"Of course there is," assented the Heir-to-Empire with the greatest dignity. "I have been one ever since I was born, and I always knew Roy belonged to me!" Then in quick impulse he ran over to the Rajput lad and flung his arms round his neck crying, "Oh Roy! Roy! I'm so glad you are my brother!"

"Not so fast, young sir," objected the sentry, who was hugely amused and interested; "what proof can you bring of this, stripling?"

Roy lifted a scared face; then hung his head.

"None, save my memory, and this mark upon my breast. My mother said we all had the stamp of truth over our hearts."

The sentry shrugged his shoulders. "That is not much in this wicked world," he said carelessly. "And anyhow it matters little if either or both of you be Kings, since ye are in cruel Kumran's power."

"Not till my Dearest-Lady returns," dissented little Akbar gravely. "Head-nurse said so; and if cruel Uncle Kumran is to get me, Dearest-Lady *won't* come back. I *know* she won't —so there!"

And, as events turned out, the Heir-to-Empire was right!

Flora Annie Steel

But a few days afterwards a messenger, bearing a blue handkerchief in his hand—the sign of death tidings to the Royal Family—appeared in hot haste before the nobles assembled in the Audience Hall.

"News! News!" he cried breathlessly. "Cover your heads with dust, ye people, while ye thank the Merciful One that Khanzada Khanum of the House of Babar hath found freedom, that after a long and godly life she hath found rest and peace. Bismillah—ul—"

The long Arabic sentence went rolling through the Hall, while Kumran stood stunned by the suddenness of his aunt's death. And yet it might have been expected; the journey was far too trying for one of her years. And she had risked it—for what?

With a rush Kumran realised that his promise still held good, and for the moment disappointment, anger, savage desire for revenge swept away his regret. Yet even he could not fail to be touched by the letter his brother Humayon had sent him by the hand of the messenger. Dearest-Lady had, he said, pled his, Kumran's, cause well, and he, Humayon, was ready to forgive for the sake of the dead woman who had loved them both, whom they both loved, and who had died with a smile.

But such softer feelings did not, could not linger long in a mind that had no fixed belief in anything. Before a day had passed the feeling that he had been tricked onto an oath he dared not break came uppermost again. Foster-father was ordered back to his damp dungeon, the little Heir-to-Empire and Roy were taken from the Palace and given over to the charge of a man noted for his hardness of heart. Only the women and little Bija, being of no account, were turned out into the streets to beg or starve as they chose.

Then followed a terrible month in which the little party were cut off from news of one another. Only Down, the cat, wandering over roofs and Heaven knows where and how, looked in here and there to settle on some one's lap and purr.

"Cats," said poor Head-nurse, as she sat opposite Foster-mother, grinding for all they were worth at a stone hand-mill in order to gain enough to keep Bija from starving, "are of all God's creatures the most contented; and so little pleases them. Hark! to Down how she purrs, just because she has found us poor miserable women."

"Allah!" replied Foster-mother more cheerfully. "Is love such a little thing? I think not, and Down hath seen my darling. Of that I feel sure; she would not come and purr otherwise."

Still it was silent comfort and there was so much going on; so much that even the "miserable women" could not hear, though they were free to come and go. But one day when Down was purring on Bija's lap in the straw thatch which was all the three had for lodging, a passer-by paused to say:

"That is the cat I used to see with the little King. Have you ought to do with him, sister?"

"I *am* his sister," replied Bija haughtily, whereat the sentry, for it was he, laughed; but for all that he paused to tell the two women what he knew; though that was not much. It could not be long, however, he said, before news of one sort or another came to them; for King Humayon was, so they said, within a day's march of Kabul, and any time they might hear the guns begin. Then would be his turn. He would fight till all was blue, and then if the outsiders won, turn round and fight for them as hardily, since all he required was plenty of fighting and plenty of food and wine.

He was right in one thing. The very next day about noon, a sudden *pouf—bing-bing—thud*, told that the first shot had been fired. And after that there was no peace and little safety. Only Foster-father in his dungeon was free even from anxiety; for fever had seized on him and he lay unconscious. And in his close prison room, where there was little air and less light, and where Roy racked his brain for stories wherewith to while away the leaden-footed hours, the little Heir-to-Empire lay listless also, yet not ill. Only weary, weary.

"I want Tumbu," he would say, "I want to run a race with him. I want to be out of doors."

And so while the city was alive with armed men, when there were assaults and repulses and sorties and forlorn hopes going on day after day, Roy would tell Mirak that some day something would happen. Some day the door would open and—

And one day the door did open. And a tall man stood for a second, half-blinded by the darkness. But the next he strode forward and caught the little Heir-to-Empire to his heart, murmuring, "My son—my little son!"

It was King Humayon; for Kumran, after pleading for a few hours' truce to allow him to make submission, had taken advantage of this breathing time to make his escape with the more desperate of his followers. Fear had overcome him once more. Having nothing in himself on which he could rely, he could not trust to the generosity of his brother.

So, after more than two and a half years of separation Akbar found his father again.

CHAPTER XVIII

THE GARDEN OF GAMES

And now, for the time at any rate, Prince Akbar's adventures were over, and all the little party prepared to enjoy themselves. Foster-father, taken out of his dungeon, soon recovered consciousness, and the news of King Humayon's victory and the Heir-to-Empire's safety, being the best tonic in the world, he was soon about again.

Head-nurse, at last absolutely restored to her proper position in Court, found, however, that her young charge had considerably outgrown the nursery. To begin with, his father, overjoyed at recovering his son, could not see too much of him, and took him about with him wherever he went.

"Time enough for his education to begin when he is four," said Humayon, when Foster-father pointed out that the boy was old beyond his years and that if he did not soon begin schooling it would be difficult for him by-and-bye.

"Let be—friend, let be!" continued the fond father; "let us have a while to amuse ourselves, now the trouble is over! I tell you I have been in such straits these last four years that I have had no time to amuse myself. Now I mean to show Kabul that life isn't so bad after all!"

Flora Annie Steel

So tall, handsome, good-natured, with a vivid love of colour and beauty and a light-heartedness almost beyond belief,— light-heartedness which had carried him through dangers that might have proved too much for one less gay—Humayon set to work to lavish his money on the most magnificent entertainments that ever were seen.

So long as winter lasted these had to be held in the Bala Hissar, where a sound of music and a ripple of laughter was to be heard day and night; but as spring began once more to carpet the barren hills with millions of flowers, Humayon's amusements went further afield. One day he and his Court, a glittering cohort of merry men, flashing with diamonds, and prepared to enjoy everything, would ride out many miles to see the great groves of Judas trees flushed with their pink blossoms; ride out to find a magnificent camp awaiting them, a magnificent repast prepared, and all the best singers and dancers in Kabul ready to amuse them. Then the next day, mayhap, they would all go a-hawking, and at each and all of these diversions Humayon's little son was part of his father's enjoyment, and so naturally, became more and more of a man every day.

He used to ride on Horse-chestnut, and Tumbu was always of the party, getting in consequence rather too fat, by reason of the rich food which was given him.

But despite all this fun and jollity little Prince Akbar was not quite satisfied.

"You took my mother away with you to the hills," he would say to his father. "Why didn't you bring her back with you? I want to see her."

Then King Humayon would laugh—for he was always merry—and bid his little son be patient. His mother would come with the spring. At present she was in Persia, but so soon as the passes were open she would start for Kabul. And then there would be fun! Whereupon little Prince Akbar would smile a dignified smile, and say, *of course* there would be fun!

Now out of this arose a plan which came into King Humayon's head, as so many other plans came, without very much thought; for he was full of kindly, not over-wise fancies. And this one was that little Prince Akbar should choose his own mother!

It would be rather a hard task for a child who had not seen her for two years and a half, and who was but a baby of less than eighteen months old when he had parted from her! But Humayon was convinced that *his* son would remember; and anyway, even if he did not, no harm would be done and it would be very amusing. So orders were given for a huge entertainment in the Arta Gardens just outside Kabul. They were the most beautiful gardens, not close cropped and orderly like English gardens, but with wide, bare, marble-paved walks and squares, big marble-stepped tanks full of waterlilies, all set in tangles of widespread roses and jasmine and gardenia. And here Humayon's fancy set up a Mystic Palace of three Houses: The House of Pleasure; The House of Fortune, and the House of Power. Never was such a beautiful Palace. By day it shone with the reflected light of thousands and thousands of looking-glasses, by night it rose outlined in every detail by thousands and thousands of little lamps. Every marble path was spread with priceless silken carpets, the very fountains were scented with attar-of-rose. All the musicians and dancers and acrobats and jugglers of Kabul were commanded to be there, snow came from the higher hills to ice the drinks, and cooks worked day and night to prepare the most wonderful dishes.

"That is what I call a King," remarked the Afghan sentry, whom Roy, going with his little master to see the preparations, found keeping guard at the gate. "None of your skinflints like Kumran. Aye!" he continued, seeing Roy's look of surprise and distaste, "I have done what I said I would—fought for Kumran till there was no more fighting to be done. And now, like His Gracious Majesty King Humayon, I am enjoying myself. I want no more! Ha! Ha!"

Little Prince Akbar, who was standing by, turned on him sharply. "Thou art a slave, fellow, and know nothing of Kingship. Roy and I do. In his country Kings ride and shoot and play polo, and—and do things. Besides," he added, "I want my mother."

"Your Highness will have to choose her then, so I hear," began the sentry almost rudely, and Roy started to rebuke him, but Prince Akbar was first.

"Of course I shall choose my own mother, slave. She is quite different, you know, from any one else in the world. Isn't she, Roy?"

The Rajput lad passed his hand over his forehead. "Mine was, Most Noble! I should know her again if I ever saw her, but I never shall."

"Say not that, boy," said the sentry, who, despite his roughness, had a kind heart and was touched by the sorrow in Roy's voice. "I have an old comrade down Suryamer way and I will speak to him of thee and see what he says; then who knows but—"

Little Akbar interrupted him gravely. "It is as God chooses. Roy always says that. Don't you, Roy?"

"By my word!" said the sentry, saluting, "you are a proper pair of Kings."

There were to be three days festival. On the first, that of Pleasure, everybody was to be dressed in white, on the second day of Power all were to be in scarlet, and on the third, the day of Fortune, the day on which little Prince Akbar was to choose his mother, every one was to wear green. Head-nurse and Foster-mother spent all their time in devising wonderful new designs for their darling's dresses, and Humayon himself added many little fanciful touches, for he had a most wonderful imagination, and this festival, which was to welcome his wife to Kabul and give her back her little son, occupied all his thoughts.

The queen arrived on the first day, but, according to custom, in a closed litter, and she went straight to the secluded balcony arranged for the royal ladies, whence she could see without being seen. So she had the advantage of her little son, who, in a magnificent costume of white and silver, looked such a darling that Queen Humeeda longed to hug him.

"Has my Amma-*jan* come?" whispered the little Prince to his father, "is she up there behind the lattice of roses?"

"Yea! she is there sure enough, little rogue," laughed Humayon. "So give a good look right through the flowers."

"No!" said little Akbar, "I've got to shut my eyes; then I can see her with my other eyes."

But his father was too busy directing the festival to hear what he said.

So the first day passed on and everybody thought it was the

very finest entertainment that ever was seen. But the second day surpassed it. The crowds, all in scarlet, filling the gardens, looked like bright roses amid the green leaves, and the blare of golden trumpets, the scattering of golden coins as *largesse*, the stately processions of soldiers made it, indeed, a marvellous show of power; and this was increased by the arrival of ambassadors from the Shah of Persia, who had so much helped King Humayon. They brought magnificent presents and hearty congratulations on success. So, nothing was lacking; and at night, lit up by red fires, the scene was one never to be forgotten. But with the dawn everything changed! A thousand servants set to work, and in one short half hour the garden showed green. Green carpets, green trees, green water falling from the fountains like liquid emeralds. And by-and-bye came green crowds, every shade of green mixing and mingling in harmony. And inside the arched pavilion of the house of Good Fortune were green rustlings of silk, green shimmerings of satin as three hundred ladies of the Court, all veiled with green veils, took their seats in a semicircle. Three hundred ladies in green all dressed alike! Which was Queen Humeeda? *That*, it was the part of a child of four to tell, a child who had not seen his mother for two and a half years!

The crowd outside, pale green, sage green, emerald green, leaf green, were hushed to silence, waiting; but from every thicket of rose and jasmine a chorus of singing birds, deftly concealed in cages behind the leaves, filled the air as Humayon and his little son advanced to take their places. The king was dressed in green also, a fine figure in royal robes embroidered with a thousand allegorical designs. He took his seat on a golden throne.

And little Prince Akbar!

He was the one spot of colour! He was the flower of the

whole garden! Dressed in rose satin of various shades, he looked indeed what Head-nurse had called him fondly, thus adding to her string of titles, "The Rose of the World."

And now the great moment approaches! The little fellow takes his stand fearlessly below his father; before him the semicircle of green veiled ladies; a hundred in the first row, a hundred in the second row, a hundred in the third row.

But little Akbar's eyes as he stands there do not wander from row to row. To tell the truth, his eyes are not open at all! He has them fast closed; for so, he knows, he can see his mother.

"Ladies! Unveil!" comes the king's voice. It sounds a little anxious.

There is a rustling of silks and satins, a faint swishing of gauze and muslins, and three hundred faces flash out, like flowers against leaves, from their green draperies.

Which is Queen Humeeda's?

For an instant the child stands silent, his lips trembling, his face flushing. Then his eyes open and he sees something.

What is it?

Is one face less smiling than another?

Where is it? In the first row, or the second row, or the third row?

What matter? There is a glad cry of—

"Amma-*jan*! My Amma-*jan*. There you are!" And a little flying figure in rose-coloured satin has dashed across the

　　　　　Flora Annie Steel

floor to fling itself into the arms of—Queen Humeeda.

Little Akbar has found his own darlingest mother, and there is not a dry eye in the whole assemblage.

CHAPTER XIX

BETWIXT CUP AND LIP

Now it may indeed seem that all our little Heir-to-Empire's troubles were over; but there is still somewhat to tell of our young hero. To begin with, Queen Humeeda was a wise woman, and she saw that it was not good for the little lad to be always at play. She knew that as a King's son in the East, he would have small time after he was ten for schooling, and as he was now close on four that did not leave many years for teaching.

So a tutor was found for him; but it is to be feared that he was by no means an industrious scholar. Indeed, we hear of such dreadful things as playing truant, so that when a day was fixed for an examination by learned men as to how the Heir-to-Empire was getting on with his studies, "at the master moment it was found that the scholar, having attired himself for sport, had disappeared!" Then his first tutor was dismissed because he encouraged his pupil in pigeon flying, and we read of his applying his thoughts more to dog-fancying and Arab horses than to his books. Still he did learn one thing, and a good thing, too.

The day he was four years and four days old he was taught, as all little Mohammedans are taught, to understand *what* he

Flora Annie Steel

was, *what* the world about him was, and to recognise that neither he himself, nor the world he lived in were the Beginning and the End of all things. It was a stately ceremonial, not beautiful, and lavish, and expensive like the Festival of the Mystic Palace, but one which left its mark for always on the mind of the child.

Despite his dislike to books as the only way of learning to be wise, he never forgot the day in the Great Mosque, when, before all his relations, he had to stand up dressed in his simple every day clothes and take the Holy Book from the hands of the high priest. And he never forgot the high priest's words:

"Read in the Name of Him who hath made all things in Heaven and earth, and Who hath given men power to be wise."

"*Bismillah!—Irruhman-nirruheem!*" he had answered as in duty bound, which means, "Thanks be to Him who is merciful in this world and merciful in the next world."

In this way young Prince Akbar learned that every man has power to be wise, and that the great mystery of birth and death is a merciful mystery.

Thus the summer passed and in early autumn King Humayon, who had now wasted nearly a whole year in amusement, found it necessary to quell rebellion in a neighbouring province.

So the governorship of Kabul was made over to a trusted noble of the Court, one Shurruf Khan by name, who was made as it were Regent for little Prince Akbar, who was left with his attendants in regal state at the palace in the Bala Hissar, while Queen Humeeda went back to India, taking

Bija with her, on a visit to her mother's relations.

Roy, whose story had become known in the Court, was now made equerry to the young prince, and very handsome he looked in his chain armour, with the noonday sun all rayed and shiny in gold on his breast, in token that he claimed to be a Sun-hero. As, indeed, seemed likely, since the Afghan sentry's old Suryamer friend had a tale about a young Rajah who had been kidnapped and, it was supposed, left in the desert to die. But whether Roy was the young Rajah or not, who could tell? They might send the story to Suryamer and see what befell. Meanwhile Roy was happy, and little Akbar and he became more and more like elder and younger brother. How much in after years the prince owed to the companionship of this friend of his childhood it is impossible to say. Perhaps it accounts for the marvellous way in which the Great Emperor Akbar ruled his Hindoo subjects.

Humayon had expected to return in a month's time, but luck was against him. A King cannot waste a whole year in amusement and so let wicked men have time to hatch plots without suffering for it. And Humayon did suffer. He had to march and counter-march with winter coming on apace, until he was struck down by sudden illness. At first the news caused no alarm, for he was known to be strong and healthy; but there came a day when folk began to whisper that the King was said to be lying unconscious, that death might come any moment.

The news stirred the whole city of Kabul to its depths. It had but lately passed into the hands of Humayon. There were not wanting many who preferred Kumran, and Kumran was in exile waiting an opportunity.

And that came with the suddenness of a summer storm. One night the gates of the town were closed by the Regent

Shurruf Khan in Humayon's name; the next dawn saw the Iron Entry, after a brief scuffle, opened in the name of Kumran! There was a rush of armed men through the streets of the town, a murder or two of loyal men in high authority. And then?

Up at the Bala Hissar, Foster-father roused from his sleep, went in haste to the Regent, expecting to hear bugles, to find troops gatherings for defence; but the gates of the Fort were open!

Shurruf Khan was traitor! He had gone over to the enemy. Ere an hour was over Kumran, scowling, walked up and down the royal apartments, a King once more; but biting his lips and frowning over something that stood between him and perfect revenge!

Foster-father, good old fool, was back in his dungeon in the well, where this time he would rot. The women, as a change, were walled up in a tiny room, where, bread and water being thrust in to them, they might eat and live, or starve and die as they chose.

But the Heir-to-Empire? What of him? Ah! fool that he had been to make that promise to a crafty old woman who had died in order to spite him. Kumran's anger rose fierce; he would have given anything to break his oath; but he could not. He was not strong enough; even his wickedness was not real.

But, short of death, the young heir should have no shelter. Kumran flung him into a miserable cell close to the Iron Gate and thought no more of him. And now, but for faithful Roy, Akbar would indeed have been in sorry plight. They had barely enough to eat, but Roy stinted himself, eating nothing but the hard half-burned crusts of the coarse hearth-cakes and excusing himself from even touching the miserable mess of pease-porridge on the ground that he did not like it. So he grew thin and his brown deer-eyes had a startled look. Indeed, he hardly slept at all, but watched and dozed beside his little master all night long.

Yet he was always cheerful. Always ready with stories and songs. When he could not remember any new-old ones, he took to inventing tales of people who were always in dangers and difficulties, but who took no notice of them, who went on their way trusting in the Truth.

"For! see you!" he would finish gravely,

"He who has Truth
Need fear no ruth."

So, ever and always his hero came out of his trials scathless.

And, by degrees, this faith in final good grew deep into both the boys' hearts, and showed in their very faces.

"By my word!" said the Afghan sentry, whom chance one day sent to guard them. "Ye be a precious pair of Kings!"

He could admire them, though he did not seem in the least ashamed of having yet once more turned his coat; for he was again on Kumran's side.

How time passed none of the prisoners cared to count. But one day the sudden roar of a great gun told them that the city was once more besieged. In truth, Humayon hearing, while still on his bed of sickness, the fatal news of Shurruf Khan's treachery, had strained every nerve, ill as he was, to come to the rescue of his little son. It was midwinter, the passes were blocked with snow, he and his troops had to meet endless

Flora Annie Steel

hardships; but at last they were before Kabul once more. Camped on the Arkaban hill, opposite the Iron Gate, the artillery were brought into position, the first shot fired.

It would take too long to follow all the varied incidents of the siege. But one thing was constant. Night after night recruits from inside the town managed to scale the walls and join King Humayon's forces. They were getting tired of Kumran, who, unable to satisfy his cruelty on the little Heir-to-Empire, vented it on all and sundry. And day by day as the number of the besieged dwindled, bit after bit of the town fell into the besiegers' hands, until at last only the Bala Hissar remained. But the Bala Hissar is a town in itself, and many a time has it withstood a siege successfully.

Now, however, it was near to the death. There could be no more talk or thought of escape. Kumran, ever half-hearted, tried it one night and failed, losing many followers in the attempt.

After that his face hardened. He went about dreaming of revenge—revenge on Humayon, even revenge on Dearest-Lady, who had tied his hands.

"Till I return!"

No! Dead folks can never return to the worldly. Even their memory comes seldom, save to the pure in heart.

And one night he hit on a plan. The fort was almost at its last gasp. All day Sumbal Khan, Humayon's famous artillery general, had been pounding away at the Iron Gate with deadly aim. A few more well-sent shots would leave the bastion crumbling, and then—

Then would come the assault through the breach, and

Kumran knew he could not face it. His force was too small.

So about midnight the door of Akbar's prison room was opened and Kumran with a few armed men stood within.

Roy, startled from a doze, was on his feet in a second.

"What want ye?" he challenged fiercely.

"Let the Hindoo fool alone," said Kumran to those who would have seized on the Rajput lad. "All we want is the child. Take him, slaves, and be quick about it."

Ere the words were out of his mouth a stalwart man bent to lift the sleeping Heir-to-Empire. Roy's sword flashed the same second, but, held back by sneering men, he was helpless.

"What want ye with him? I say, what want ye with him?" panted the poor lad as he struggled madly.

Kumran paused at the door to turn an icy cold look of cruelty upon him. "What! Thou wouldst know? Then thou shalt have it, young idolater. It may cool thy hot blood. I will dress him in dust colour like the walls of Kabul and hang him over the battlement at dawn as a mark for my brother's artillery. Then we shall see the breach in my citadel made! Then we shall see my revenge—but it will not be of my making! His father shall kill him."

So with a mirthless laugh he followed his men, who were bearing away the Heir-to-Empire, still but half awake.

Roy stood for one second like a stone, too horror stricken for full belief; but the echoing laugh convinced him; with a wild cry he rushed to the narrow window and shook fruitlessly at its iron bars like a wild animal when it is newly caged. But they were immovable.

Yet something must be done—something—something—

The thought of dawn was too dreadful. The beautiful, calm, peaceful April dawn, shadowy grey! Just light enough to see the outline of the Bala Hissar, just light enough to begin upon the breach once more; but too dark to see what was in the line of fire.

Yes! Something must be done, and done swiftly. Not four hours left before the eastern hills would begin to show dark against the coming of day.

CHAPTER XX

ESCAPED

Once more Roy felt helpless and hopeless before the great task which seemed to be laid upon him. He alone out of all the little Heir-to-Empire's guardians knew the dire danger he was in. Yet how could he, a poor, prisoned Rajput lad, save the young prince?

Still he had to be saved; he must be saved; and there was no time to be lost. At dawn the firing would recommence from the Arkaban hill; at dawn the helpless child would be in the half-breached bastion exposed to that fire!

Yes! He, Roy, must get out somehow. If he could only loosen one bar of the window so that he could squeeze through, then he might be able to let himself down by a rope twined out of his long waist-cloth and turban! Thus he might be able to get out of the fort! He might be able to gain the camp on the Arkaban hill before dawn! So he might be able to warn the guns not to fire on the bastion; might be able to tell them that the Heir-to-Empire hung there!

What a number of "might be ables"; but would he be able, even for the first task?

Flora Annie Steel

He took up his sword and began forthwith on the iron bar; but the mortar was hard, he could scarcely make a mark upon it. Still, it must be done. In order to free his arms better for the work he took off all his clothes save his flimsy, sleeveless waistcoat and the loin-cloth that was girt about him, and buckled down steadily. But when more than an hour had passed the bar seemed as firm as ever. As he crouched down on the window sill he could see through it to the flat roof of the neighboring palaces; for it was a bright moonlight night still, though the moon must be nigh to her setting. So the thought crossed his mind that if he could only squeeze through he might be able to reach one of those roofs; since, if he remembered aright, a wide cornice ran just below. He paused for a second in his labour to see if this was so, craning his head through the crossbars. Yes, the cornice was there! Scarcely wide enough for a cat to walk, but if he got through in time he would risk it. He must risk it!

But would he get through in time? He set to work again feverishly until suddenly a familiar sound reached his ear from outside; the sound of a cat purring!

Could it be Down? She had not found them out in their new prison, but if she had happened to be on the roof when he looked out of the window she might have seen him or smelled him—yes! There was a white cat on the cornice, and the next moment Down was on the sill, arching her back and purring away contentedly.

So she had found them at last—no! not *them*, for the Heir-to-Empire was not there—he had been stolen away! Roy could have leaned his head on Down's soft fur and cried his heart out in despair at his own helplessness, but he set his teeth instead and dug harder with the sword point.

Would the bar never loosen? So the minutes passed without

a sound save the grating of the eager sword and the soft, soothing purr of the cat as she sat beside him watching him indifferently. Then suddenly the latter ceased and Down leaped swiftly to the floor of the cell. Doubtless she heard something. Cats hear so many things humans do not hear, and they seem to know so many things humans do not know, so perhaps she heard a mouse far down the arched passage, or even in the next cell. Anyhow she marched straight to the door and stood by it, *miaowing* to be let out. Ah! if he only could let her out! If the door were only open, thought poor Roy, as he worked away at the still immovable bar.

"No! Down, no! I can't," he murmured bitterly as the cat *miaowed* more and more insistently.

But still the *miaowing* went on. Down became quite plaintive, then ill-used; finally she leaped onto Roy's shoulder, licked his ear with her rough red tongue as if to coax him, and was back again at the door asking to be let out.

Why was she so set on it? Roy turned to look at her half stupidly and for a moment forgot his task; forgot how rapidly time was passing; forgot everything save that Down was asking to be let out. So wearily he passed to the door, and scarcely conscious of what he was doing, laid his hand on the latch.

"I can't, Down," he said; "I can't open—" He broke off hurriedly.

For the latch yielded, the door opened!!

It could never have been locked!!

Had they forgotten, or, having secured the Heir-to-Empire, had they not cared what became of the henchman? The latter,

Flora Annie Steel

most likely, for there was no sentry in the arched passage along which Down had already disappeared.

Another second and Roy, sword in hand, had disappeared down it also, remembering as he ran a certain little fretted marble balcony which gave on the gardens below. For Roy, of course, knew every turn of the Bala Hissar. This balcony opened onto an unused gallery room. To gain this, bolt the heavy door behind him, and so, secure from interruption, set to work twining a rope from strips torn from his turban and waistband did not take long; but it was a good twenty minutes before he had knotted all fast; though while he worked he thought of nothing else; of nothing but somehow reaching the garden. Once there he would face the next difficulty. One was enough at a time. And then, when he had made the rope fast to one of the marble pillars and slid down it, it proved too short. He swung with his feet just touching the topmost branch of a blossoming peach tree. There was nothing for it but to let go, snatch at the branches as he fell and trust to chance for safety. He found it; and dropped to the ground amid a perfect shower of shed peach petals.

So he stood for an instant to consider what must come next. A gate! Aye! but which? The farthest from the point of attack would be the best, as there would be less vigilance there. That meant the Delhi gate, and meant also a long round; yet he must be quick, for already there was a faint lightening of the eastern sky. But the moon had set and the shadows, always darker in the hour before dawn, lay upon all things.

And luckily he knew every turn of the Bala Hissar garden, knew every point where danger might be expected. So he began to make his way carefully. He dodged more than one sentry by creeping on through the bushes while the man passed away from him, and crouched among them, still as a mouse, while the measured march came toward him. And once he had to run for bare life from a shower of arrows which a company of soldiers sent into the darkness after a suspicious rustling in the bushes. But mostly the men on duty had too much to think of outside the walls to trouble themselves much about the things inside them.

So with doublings and turnings he came at last on the Delhi gate, a small, round, flat-roofed building pierced by a high archway. It was too dark for him to see its outline, but he knew it well, and paused against the outside wall to consider what he had to do next. The place seemed almost deserted, but a glimmer of light from the archway and the even tramp of a sentry's footstep told it was not all unguarded.

What was he to do? It would be useless for him to try and steal past the sentry, as the gate beyond must be locked, or at any rate bolted and barred. He must either, therefore, try and overpower the man or else try to gain the flat roof by the stairs—of which he knew the position—and, trusting to find a rope or something of the sort in the upper room of the gate, let himself down into the ditch outside.

Now, Roy was a well-grown lad of nigh fifteen, tall for his age, and with his light, youthful sinews of iron might well be a match for many a man, especially as his purpose was like steel, and that is ever half the battle. But there was the chance of other soldiers being within call, and that might mean failure. Now, *that* must not be. Roy had to succeed— he must!

Therefore the roof was the wiser, safer plan; he must make for the stairs, trusting to escape notice when the sentry's back was turned. Till then—silence!

But even as he settled this in his mind Fate was against him.

As he crouched in the darkness something cold suddenly touched his face, and the next moment a clamour of excited yappings and joyful barks arose, as something warm and furry and cold and slobbery flung itself all over him.

Tumbu! It could be nothing but blundering, bumbling Tumbu! He made one useless effort to still the dog, then rose to his feet feeling himself discovered, prepared to run for it. But it was too late. A sentry, lantern in hand, roused by the commotion, barred the way. All seemed lost, but a ray of hope shone when the familiar voice of the Afghan sentry, the unrepentant turncoat, was heard as the lantern waved in Roy's very face.

"By my word, one of the Kings! How come you hither at this time o' night, friend?"

The voice was a little thick, as if the owner, finding the quiet of the Delhi Gate wearisome, had sought amusement in a skin of wine.

Roy gave a gasp—he was too confused for thought. "The dog—" he began.

"Aye! The dog that was yours and is mine," jeered the sentry. "So he nosed you out, did he? Knows his duty—good dog, Tumbu! Knows his master now! Knows who saved him from starvation when he was lurking about in the gutter. Eh! you brute!"

He lunged a kick at Tumbu, who retreated a step, looking from the new to the old master, feeling, in truth, a trifle confused. For the Afghan sentry had certainly found him homeless, friendless, and the dog had stuck by him, feeling that here at least was something vaguely connected with the past life. But now he stood doubtful, expectant, his little ears pricked, his small eyes watchful.

"Well," continued the sentry with a half-drunken laugh, "dog or no dog, you've no business here, so come along with me, my King."

He reached out a heavy hand, and Roy shrunk from it. As he did so there came a sound which sent the blood to Roy's heart with a spasm of instant hope, of possible escape. It was Tumbu's low growl as he realised that some one wanted to touch his old master and that his old master did not want to be touched.

"At him, Tumbu! At him, good dog!" The words came to Roy in a flash, and like a flash the great, powerful dog leaped forward, his fur a-bristle, his white teeth gleaming, and the next instant, taken by the suddenness of the attack, the sentry lay on his back half stunned by the fall, while Tumbu, on the top of him, checked even a cry by a clutch at his throat. A soft clutch so far; but one that would tear through flesh if needful.

Roy was on his knees beside the fallen man.

"Hist! not a sound or the dog shall kill you. He can. Give me the keys. I want to get out of the gate! The keys, do you hear?"

The sentry tried to struggle, but warned by the weight of the dog on his breast and those sharp teeth ready to close upon his throat, murmured hoarsely, "It is only barred, but the bolts are difficult. If you will let me get up and call off your dog—"

But Roy took no heed of his words. "Keep him there, Tumbu," he whispered as he ran to the gate.

Flora Annie Steel

Bolted and barred it was, and in the darkness of the archway it was hard to see, for the lantern had gone out in the scuffle. But there was no time to lose, for already beyond the archway it showed faintly light. One bar down! The sentry made a faint effort to stir, that was answered by an ominous growl from Tumbu.

Only one more bolt now!

Roy's long fingers were at it—his whole strength went to it—it creaked—groaned—slid, and with a sob of exultation Roy felt the fresh air of dawn in his face as he stood outside the Bala Hissar.

But he had still much to do. The city must be skirted, the hill of Arkaban gained, and already a faint primrose streak in the eastern sky told of coming light.

CHAPTER XXI

DAWN

Upon the Arkaban hill the artillery men were already at work. In those days guns were not what they are now, quick loading, quick firing.

It needed a good hour to ram the coarse powder down, adjust the round ball and prepare the priming; to say nothing of the task of aiming. So, long ere dawn, the glimmering lights were seen about the battery, which, perched on a hill, gave on the half-breached bastion. Between the two stretched an open space of undulating ground. Sumbal, "the master fireworker," as he is called in the old history books, was up betimes seeing to his men, and with him came a grave, silent man, who, though he had no interest in the quarrels of Humayon and his brothers, was as eager as any to get within the walls of Kabul and find what he sought—a Rajput lad of whom word had been brought to a little half-desert Rajput state lying far away in the Jesulmer plain.

For the grave, silent man, who showed so much knowledge of warfare, who was keen to see everything new in weapons and the handling of them, was a messenger sent by a widowed mother to see if indeed it could be her long-lost son, of whom a certain old trooper had spoken on his return

176　　　　　　　　　Flora Annie Steel

from Kabul.

"See you!" said Sumbal, who was a bit of a boaster, "give me time to aim and I'll warrant me 'Thunder of God'" (that was the name let in with gold on the breech of the gun) "will hit the mark within a yard every time. Thou shalt see it ere-long. There is a sort of pigeon place on the face of the bastion where I will aim, and thou shalt see the splinters of it spin!" He shaded his eyes with his hand and looked piercingly into the shadows. "'Tis too dark to see it yet, but so soon as it shows I will let fly, and then—"

And then?

Roy, who had never stopped for a breath yet in his headlong race, was at that very moment rounding on the bastion, and looking up, saw what he had feared to see—a little figure bound hand and foot to a framework of wood that hung close to what Sumbal had called the pigeon place, seeming to form part of it. The child was not crying. Perhaps he was past that. Perhaps he had never cried, but had taken this last and urgent danger as he had taken others, with grave dignity.

All we know is that he hung there on the wall, and that before his very eyes the light was growing in the east, and over in the hill battery a dozen men were sweating away to bring the "Thunder of God" into position. Roy gave a gasp. Should he call to the little Heir-to-Empire and let him know that a friend was near, that help might come? No! perhaps he did not realise his danger. It was better to let be.

So gathering all his forces for a last effort, he dashed into the open for the final five minutes' run. And there could be no dodging here. Every loophole of the bastion was, he knew, crammed with the matchlocks of many marksmen. And there was now, worse luck, little darkness to cover him!

"Three minutes more, friend!" said Sumbal boastfully, "and thou shalt see what thou wilt see. Slave! the port fire, quick. I will give the signal. Lo! What is up?"

A rattle of musketry rose on the still air of dawn, and an artillery man leaned over the low embrasure to see better into the intervening valley.

"Some one escaping," he said with a yawn, for he had been up half the night. "Lo! he runs like a hare! But they will have him, for sure."

"Quick," called Sumbal, "we will silence their noise. The portfire, I say. I will fire old Thunderer myself."

The man carrying the flaming flashlight handed it to his superior, but in so doing by some mischance it dropped, and in the dropping went out!

"Fool!" cried Sumbal passionately. "Are we to stand insulted here without reply while thou fetchest another? Put him in irons, sergeant, and bring light at once!"

But the grave, silent Rajput was watching the runner. "He is but a boy," he said slowly, "yet see how he runs. And they have hit him, for he staggers. Yet he comes on. He must bring news, friend, for sure!"

"News!" echoed Sumbal contemptuously; "we have half a hundred such runaways coming in every day. It is no news that King Humayon is better liked than Kumran. Lo! hast thou it at last?" He snatched the portfire from the sergeant and went toward the gun.

"Stay one moment, friend!" said the grave and silent man with sudden command in his voice. "A moment's hastiness

Flora Annie Steel

may bring disaster. Discretion is better than valour. Yonder boy brings news—he waves his arms—he shouts! Stay at least till we can hear what he says."

Sumbal laughed. "Bah! But, see you, I stay my hand while I count ten—no more."

"One! two! three! four!"

The artillery men, amused at the race, leaned over. "He runs well!—He will win!—He will lose!—He climbs like a hill cat!"—

"*Five! six! seven! eight! nine!*"

And now, unintelligible from sheer breathlessness, Roy's voice is heard. The grave, silent Rajput leaps out to meet him.

"*Ten!*"

Sumbal's hand swings the portfire to the breech.

Roy sees it, throws up his arms wildly, and with a cry—

"The bastion! The bastion! The Heir-to-Empire!" falls head-long into the Rajput's arms.

"What did he say?" asked the master fireworker, pausing half surprised, half angry.

But the Rajput was too busy tearing aside Roy's flimsy, bloodstained waistcoat to answer.

"Something about the bastion and the Heir-to-Empire, master!" said the sergeant doubtfully. "Mayhap 'twould be as well to wait till we can see more clearly. Kumran," he added in a lower voice, "would stick at naught—"

Sumbal hesitated, then put down the portfire and walked over to the fallen lad, beside whom the stranger was kneeling.

"He is not dead! He is not dead!" said the grave, silent Rajput, looking up, his face working, the tears streaming down his bronzed cheek. "My master is not dead!"

"Who?" asked Sumbal, uncomprehending.

"I knew it must be he!" went on the man exultantly, even in his grief. "None could do that sort of thing save a Sun hero! My Master! my King! See, here the race mark on his breast! The sign of uttermost truth! My Master! My King!"

But Roy did not hear himself called thus. He did not even know for days afterwards if he had succeeded or if he had failed; for a wound just above the heart, close to the sign-mark of his race, very nearly carried him off into the Shadowy Land where all things are remembered, yet all are forgotten.

But he *had* succeeded. He had saved the Heir-to-Empire's life that dawn, and a day or two afterwards Kumran, daily more hated for his cruelty, had escaped, and the soldiers, rejoiced to get rid of him, flung open the gates of the Bala Hissar, thus ending Prince Akbar's adventures.

But when Roy came to himself Mirak was sitting beside him and Down was purring on Bija's lap; Bija, who had just returned from India with Queen Humeeda in time to console the Heir-to-Empire for all he must have suffered during the few days he was left alone with cruel Uncle Kumran. How much he had suffered no one knew, and the little fellow refused to say anything about it. It was a way he had when the luck went against him. So, just as he had remarked when he had fallen down the ravine, when the white cat and the black dog first came to him, that he had "tumbu-down," so now he simply said that it wasn't "very comfy," but that Tumbu had come to see him more than once. And this was possible, for you may be sure that once he allowed the Afghan sentry to rise, Tumbu, being a wise dog, never went near him again. Therefore he *had* to find his old master.

And Foster-father, Foster-mother and Head-nurse were all there, the latter greatly subdued for the time, and in her gratitude to Roy inclined to give him some of the titles she was wont to bestow on little Prince Akbar.

For there was no doubt whatever that the lad was the rightful Rajah of Suryamer, whom wicked rebels had exposed in the desert to die, who had been found and kept alive by wandering goatherds and had finally been discovered when unconscious from sunstroke by the royal fugitives.

And out of this arose the only sadness of the happy May days when the little party once more journeyed out to Babar's tomb towards evening to sit under the *arghawan* trees and watch the sunset.

Of course Dearest-Lady was not there, but all the others were assembled, and Down, the cat, purred as loud as ever, while Tumbu, the dog, frolicked round even more like a golliwog than before. But it was not the absence of the Khanzada Khanum which made faces thoughtful at times. She, they knew, was at rest, and they laid flowers for her beside those they gathered in memory of Firdoos Gita Makani—on whom be peace!

No! it was the knowledge that Roy could not remain with them. So soon as he was strong again he must go back to his mother, go back to a people who, tired of rebellion, were longing for their old rulers.

"You see, brother, I am a King," said Roy sorrowfully, "and Kings cannot always do what they like."

"Do you think they ever do, *really*?" asked the little Heir-to-Empire gravely, "for I don't."

And here we come to the end—for a time at least—of Prince Akbar's adventures.

Now, if you want to know how much of this so-called veracious story is really true, I cannot quite say.

Did some one like Roy *really* tell the master fireworker that the Heir-to-Empire was hung over the battlements of the bastion? If some one did not, how did the master-fireworker find it out? And he did; indeed, in the history books he takes great credit to himself for *having* found it out. But then he was a boaster.

Then did Dearest-Lady really bind Kumran by an oath not to harm the Heir-to-Empire until she returned?

If she did not, then why did she, an old, frail woman of seventy, go out into the wilderness just as winter was coming on, and why did not cruel Kumran kill the Heir-to-Empire when he had him in his power?

These are all questions; but what is certain is that Baby Akbar did go through all these adventures before he was five years old.

Flora Annie Steel

So good-bye, brave little lads! Good-bye, stout old Foster-father and kindly Foster-mother! Good-bye, worthy Head-nurse with your strings of titles, and good-bye, dainty little Bija! Good-bye also to grinning Meroo, to purring Down, and frolicking Tumbu!

And for those other three whose memory remained—Old Faithful, Dearest Lady, and the Great Emperor, Firdoos Gita Makani, who all helped the little prince to safety, what of them?

"Heaven," as the marble slab among the tulips and violets of the Garden-of-the-New-Year says,

"'Is their eternal abode.'"

Choose from Thousands of 1stWorldLibrary Classics By

A. M. Barnard
Ada Leverson
Adolphus William Ward
Aesop
Agatha Christie
Alexander Aaronsohn
Alexander Kielland
Alexandre Dumas
Alfred Gatty
Alfred Ollivant
Alice Duer Miller
Alice Turner Curtis
Alice Dunbar
Allen Chapman
Alleyne Ireland
Ambrose Bierce
Amelia E. Barr
Amory H. Bradford
Andrew Lang
Andrew McFarland Davis
Andy Adams
Angela Brazil
Anna Alice Chapin
Anna Sewell
Annie Besant
Annie Hamilton Donnell
Annie Payson Call
Annie Roe Carr
Annonaymous
Anton Chekhov
Archibald Lee Fletcher
Arnold Bennett
Arthur C. Benson
Arthur Conan Doyle
Arthur M. Winfield
Arthur Ransome
Arthur Schnitzler
Arthur Train
Atticus
B.H. Baden-Powell
B. M. Bower
B. C. Chatterjee
Baroness Emmuska Orczy
Baroness Orczy
Basil King
Bayard Taylor
Ben Macomber
Bertha Muzzy Bower
Bjornstjerne Bjornson

Booth Tarkington
Boyd Cable
Bram Stoker
C. Collodi
C. E. Orr
C. M. Ingleby
Carolyn Wells
Catherine Parr Traill
Charles A. Eastman
Charles Amory Beach
Charles Dickens
Charles Dudley Warner
Charles Farrar Browne
Charles Ives
Charles Kingsley
Charles Klein
Charles Hanson Towne
Charles Lathrop Pack
Charles Romyn Dake
Charles Whibley
Charles Willing Beale
Charlotte M. Braeme
Charlotte M. Yonge
Charlotte Perkins Stetson
Clair W. Hayes
Clarence Day Jr.
Clarence E. Mulford
Clemence Housman
Confucius
Coningsby Dawson
Cornelis DeWitt Wilcox
Cyril Burleigh
D. H. Lawrence
Daniel Defoe
David Garnett
Dinah Craik
Don Carlos Janes
Donald Keyhoe
Dorothy Kilner
Dougan Clark
Douglas Fairbanks
E. Nesbit
E. P. Roe
E. Phillips Oppenheim
E. S. Brooks
Earl Barnes
Edgar Rice Burroughs
Edith Van Dyne
Edith Wharton

Edward Everett Hale
Edward J. O'Biren
Edward S. Ellis
Edwin L. Arnold
Eleanor Atkins
Eleanor Hallowell Abbott
Eliot Gregory
Elizabeth Gaskell
Elizabeth McCracken
Elizabeth Von Arnim
Ellem Key
Emerson Hough
Emilie F. Carlen
Emily Bronte
Emily Dickinson
Enid Bagnold
Enilor Macartney Lane
Erasmus W. Jones
Ernie Howard Pie
Ethel May Dell
Ethel Turner
Ethel Watts Mumford
Eugene Sue
Eugenie Foa
Eugene Wood
Eustace Hale Ball
Evelyn Everett-green
Everard Cotes
F. H. Cheley
F. J. Cross
F. Marion Crawford
Fannie E. Newberry
Federick Austin Ogg
Ferdinand Ossendowski
Fergus Hume
Florence A. Kilpatrick
Fremont B. Deering
Francis Bacon
Francis Darwin
Frances Hodgson Burnett
Frances Parkinson Keyes
Frank Gee Patchin
Frank Harris
Frank Jewett Mather
Frank L. Packard
Frank V. Webster
Frederic Stewart Isham
Frederick Trevor Hill
Frederick Winslow Taylor

Friedrich Kerst
Friedrich Nietzsche
Fyodor Dostoyevsky
G.A. Henty
G.K. Chesterton
Gabrielle E. Jackson
Garrett P. Serviss
Gaston Leroux
George A. Warren
George Ade
Geroge Bernard Shaw
George Cary Eggleston
George Durston
George Ebers
George Eliot
George Gissing
George MacDonald
George Meredith
George Orwell
George Sylvester Viereck
George Tucker
George W. Cable
George Wharton James
Gertrude Atherton
Gordon Casserly
Grace E. King
Grace Gallatin
Grace Greenwood
Grant Allen
Guillermo A. Sherwell
Gulielma Zollinger
Gustav Flaubert
H. A. Cody
H. B. Irving
H. C. Bailey
H. G. Wells
H. H. Munro
H. Irving Hancock
H. R. Naylor
H. Rider Haggard
H. W. C. Davis
Haldeman Julius
Hall Caine
Hamilton Wright Mabie
Hans Christian Andersen
Harold Avery
Harold McGrath
Harriet Beecher Stowe
Harry Castlemon
Harry Coghill
Harry Houidini

Hayden Carruth
Helent Hunt Jackson
Helen Nicolay
Hendrik Conscience
Hendy David Thoreau
Henri Barbusse
Henrik Ibsen
Henry Adams
Henry Ford
Henry Frost
Henry James
Henry Jones Ford
Henry Seton Merriman
Henry W Longfellow
Herbert A. Giles
Herbert Carter
Herbert N. Casson
Herman Hesse
Hildegard G. Frey
Homer
Honore De Balzac
Horace B. Day
Horace Walpole
Horatio Alger Jr.
Howard Pyle
Howard R. Garis
Hugh Lofting
Hugh Walpole
Humphry Ward
Ian Maclaren
Inez Haynes Gillmore
Irving Bacheller
Isabel Cecilia Williams
Isabel Hornibrook
Israel Abrahams
Ivan Turgenev
J. G.Austin
J. Henri Fabre
J. M. Barrie
J. M. Walsh
J. Macdonald Oxley
J. R. Miller
J. S. Fletcher
J. S. Knowles
J. Storer Clouston
J. W. Duffield
Jack London
Jacob Abbott
James Allen
James Andrews
James Baldwin

James Branch Cabell
James DeMille
James Joyce
James Lane Allen
James Lane Allen
James Oliver Curwood
James Oppenheim
James Otis
James R. Driscoll
Jane Abbott
Jane Austen
Jane L. Stewart
Janet Aldridge
Jens Peter Jacobsen
Jerome K. Jerome
Jessie Graham Flower
John Buchan
John Burroughs
John Cournos
John F. Kennedy
John Gay
John Glasworthy
John Habberton
John Joy Bell
John Kendrick Bangs
John Milton
John Philip Sousa
John Taintor Foote
Jonas Lauritz Idemil Lie
Jonathan Swift
Joseph A. Altsheler
Joseph Carey
Joseph Conrad
Joseph E. Badger Jr
Joseph Hergesheimer
Joseph Jacobs
Jules Vernes
Julian Hawthrone
Julie A Lippmann
Justin Huntly McCarthy
Kakuzo Okakura
Karle Wilson Baker
Kate Chopin
Kenneth Grahame
Kenneth McGaffey
Kate Langley Bosher
Kate Langley Bosher
Katherine Cecil Thurston
Katherine Stokes
L. A. Abbot
L. T. Meade

L. Frank Baum
Latta Griswold
Laura Dent Crane
Laura Lee Hope
Laurence Housman
Lawrence Beasley
Leo Tolstoy
Leonid Andreyev
Lewis Carroll
Lewis Sperry Chafer
Lilian Bell
Lloyd Osbourne
Louis Hughes
Louis Joseph Vance
Louis Tracy
Louisa May Alcott
Lucy Fitch Perkins
Lucy Maud Montgomery
Luther Benson
Lydia Miller Middleton
Lyndon Orr
M. Corvus
M. H. Adams
Margaret E. Sangster
Margret Howth
Margaret Vandercook
Margaret W. Hungerford
Margret Penrose
Maria Edgeworth
Maria Thompson Daviess
Mariano Azuela
Marion Polk Angellotti
Mark Overton
Mark Twain
Mary Austin
Mary Catherine Crowley
Mary Cole
Mary Hastings Bradley
Mary Roberts Rinehart
Mary Rowlandson
M. Wollstonecraft Shelley
Maud Lindsay
Max Beerbohm
Myra Kelly
Nathaniel Hawthrone
Nicolo Machiavelli
O. F. Walton
Oscar Wilde
Owen Johnson
P.G. Wodehouse
Paul and Mabel Thorne

Paul G. Tomlinson
Paul Severing
Percy Brebner
Percy Keese Fitzhugh
Peter B. Kyne
Plato
Quincy Allen
R. Derby Holmes
R. L. Stevenson
R. S. Ball
Rabindranath Tagore
Rahul Alvares
Ralph Bonehill
Ralph Henry Barbour
Ralph Victor
Ralph Waldo Emmerson
Rene Descartes
Ray Cummings
Rex Beach
Rex E. Beach
Richard Harding Davis
Richard Jefferies
Richard Le Gallienne
Robert Barr
Robert Frost
Robert Gordon Anderson
Robert L. Drake
Robert Lansing
Robert Lynd
Robert Michael Ballantyne
Robert W. Chambers
Rosa Nouchette Carey
Rudyard Kipling
Saint Augustine
Samuel B. Allison
Samuel Hopkins Adams
Sarah Bernhardt
Sarah C. Hallowell
Selma Lagerlof
Sherwood Anderson
Sigmund Freud
Standish O'Grady
Stanley Weyman
Stella Benson
Stella M. Francis
Stephen Crane
Stewart Edward White
Stijn Streuvels
Swami Abhedananda
Swami Parmananda
T. S. Ackland

T. S. Arthur
The Princess Der Ling
Thomas A. Janvier
Thomas A Kempis
Thomas Anderton
Thomas Bailey Aldrich
Thomas Bulfinch
Thomas De Quincey
Thomas Dixon
Thomas H. Huxley
Thomas Hardy
Thomas More
Thornton W. Burgess
U. S. Grant
Upton Sinclair
Valentine Williams
Various Authors
Vaughan Kester
Victor Appleton
Victor G. Durham
Victoria Cross
Virginia Woolf
Wadsworth Camp
Walter Camp
Walter Scott
Washington Irving
Wilbur Lawton
Wilkie Collins
Willa Cather
Willard F. Baker
William Dean Howells
William le Queux
W. Makepeace Thackeray
William W. Walter
William Shakespeare
Winston Churchill
Yei Theodora Ozaki
Yogi Ramacharaka
Young E. Allison
Zane Grey

www.ingramcontent.com/pod-product-compliance
Lightning Source LLC
Chambersburg PA
CBHW031349170626
46807CB00002B/888